JAVANESE SILAT

JAVANESE SILAT

The Fighting Art of Perisai Diri

QUINTIN CHAMBERS
DONN F. DRAEGER

KODANSHA INTERNATIONAL LTD.
Tokyo, New York and San Francisco

Distributed in the United States by Kodansha International/USA, Ltd. through Harper & Row, Publishers, Inc., 10 East 53rd Street, New York, New York 10022. In Canada by Fitzhenry & Whiteside Ltd., 150 Lesmill Road, Don Mills, Ontario M3B 2T6. In Mexico and Central America by Harla S.A. de C.V., Apartado 30–456, Mexico 4, D.F. In South America by Harper & Row, International Department. In the United Kingdom by Phaidon Press Ltd., Littlegate House, St. Ebbe's Street, Oxford OX1 1SQ. In Europe by Boxerbooks, Inc., Limmatstrasse 111, 8031 Zurich. In Australia and New Zealand by Bookwise (Australia) Pty. Ltd., 104–8 Sussex Street, Sydney 2000. In the Far East by Toppan Company (S) Pte. Ltd., No. 38, Liu Fang Road, Jurong, Singapore 22.

Published by Kodansha International Ltd., 2–12–21 Otowa, Bunkyo-ku, Tokyo 112 and Kodansha International /USA, Ltd., 10 East 53rd Street, New York, New York 10022 and 44 Montgomery Street, San Francisco, California 94104.

Printed in Japan.

LCC 78–60969
ISBN 0–87011–353–4
JBC 2075–786821–2361

First edition, 1978

TABLE OF CONTENTS

PREFACE

Centuries old, the Javanese art of self-defense called *silat* is a repository of primordial cultural consciousness and is living proof of the spirit of Javanese syncretism. Several hundred different types of silat systems are now practiced throughout Indonesia, each with its own unity, coherence, and history; collectively, the systems play important roles in the lives of countless thousands of people. Java itself has a substantial share of silat systems, some centuries old, others quite modern.

The purpose of this introductory study is to offer, in both their mechanical and spiritual dimensions, the technical characteristics of Silat Perisai Diri, which was developed in central and east Java. This kind of silat has been selected by the authors because it represents a typically indigenous Javanese effort to bridge the cultural distance between the ancient past and the modern Indonesian nation-state. No special knowledge is required to read this book, though the authors do presume that their readers will have a searching interest in the art of hand-to-hand combat in self-defense, a subject as relevant today in our modern world as it was at any time in history.

Special thanks are due to R. M. S. Dirdjoatmodjo, the founder of Silat Perisai Diri, and to his three assistant instructors, Ruddy Johnny Kapojos, Suparjono, and I. Made Swetja, whose enthusiasm, cooperation, and technical skills have made this book possible. The photographic processing skills of Ichiro Kobayashi and his staff are also much appreciated.

1 THE SILAT LEGEND AND ITS PRACTICAL MEANING

The Malay peoples who inhabit the lands that today comprise Indonesia, Singapore, Malaysia, and the southernmost regions of the Philippines and Thailand (on the Isthmus of Kra) all regard the combative art of *silat* as an indigenous creation. Many different legends have arisen to offer some explanation of the exact nature and source of the inspiration that led to the original silat system. Some of these legends have been incorporated into Malay folk tales and are well known to all Malays. To this day they are being passed on to successive generations by the medium of oral tradition.

Our intention in this chapter is neither to relate these different legends nor to analyze and evaluate them. The legends not only disagree about the circumstances behind the founding of silat, but also establish different geographical locations in which the founding is said to have taken place. Rather, we shall take up what is perhaps the best known of these legends—stripped of its proper names and time and place identifications—in the hope that it will give to the users of this book what it has given to silat combatants from the beginning: a vital cosmic scheme offering powerful intellectual stimulation and guiding moral principles.

> A Malay youth crouched at the edge of a jungle pool over which hung the branches of a huge flowering tree. One of the tree's blossoms fluttered acrobatically downward and quietly alighted on the surface of the water near the place where the lad was located. As he watched, the flower began to move with light, evasive actions along a strong current caused by water plunging from a waterfall at one end of the pool. The floating blossom sped with increasing rapidity toward the powerful vortex being generated by the plunging water. Then, as it neared the base of the violent cascade, it

suddenly swerved away from what appeared to the youth to be its certain destruction. The spray of the waterfall rebounding from the surface of the pool was generating a countercurrent that flowed with sufficient force away from the vortex to send the flower back out into the main current. Time and time again this process was repeated.

The youth watched intently as the flower moved from a position of safety to one of imminent danger, and then surely back again to the safety of mid-pool. His curiosity now fully aroused, the excited youth scooped the flower from the water and found to his great surprise that it was totally undamaged. Here indeed, he thought, was a miraculous natural principle —simple, effective, and worthy of some application in human life.

We are further informed by the legend that the inspiration the youth received from the manner in which the flower avoided destruction gave rise to the development of the core principle for the technical base of the Malay system of combat that came to be called silat. There is no legitimate reason to doubt the occurrence of the events that the legend depicts, but the story is probably an anachronism selected to establish ethnic, temporal, and spatial identity for the origin of Malay silat. The structural form of the legend, however, can be readily accepted as being descriptive of silat's technical base.

The theory of silat technique hinges on the principle of economy of force and energy. The silat exponent must utilize his physical and spiritual energies to his best advantage when confronted by an assailant. In practice he seeks to reduce any advantage that the assailant may have, or seek to apply, through the use of efficient stance-posture combinations and clever maneuvers. Silat is characterized by its evasiveness. The exponent always depends on his great agility, that is, the adaptability of his mind and body—flexibility in its fullest sense—to meet situations thrust upon him. He specializes in developing an instant and appropriate reaction to crises, and all physical movement stemming therefrom is made in a light, elusive manner in preference to the application of resistive brute force.

As important as are the mechanical elements of silat, it is the ethical concept that is given higher regard by all exponents of the art. Like the flower in the legend that responded to the forces of water currents in the pool, the silat exponent is always responsive to solicited or imposed aggression, never overtly offensive; he will not take the first opportunity to launch an attack against another person or persons. This apparently pacific outlook, however, requires careful qualification in its interpretation.

Should the silat exponent be set upon directly by an aggressor, his response will come about naturally and as an easily identifiable "defensive" response. He acts only after the attacker's first physical move and because of it. But when the silat exponent faces an individual who has not yet made any physical move to attack and who merely harbors aggressive intentions, the matter of who is defensive and who is offensive is not so obvious. In this case, if the silat exponent suspects that an attack is imminent he is then privileged by silat ethics to take the initiative. He may take decisive action and need not wait for the first blow to be struck by the other party. In the view of silat ethics the exponent is, in this case, still acting defensively in response to an attack. The exercise of this prerogative is based on the belief that sufficient combative training has given the exponent an infallible degree of sensitivity to aggressive intent in another person. It is this supraliminal attribute of the trained exponent that keeps the prerogative from becoming an excuse for launching unwarranted aggression.

In silat the timing of the attack initiative, which determines who gains combative advantage through an action taken appropriate to the situation, is a broad matter that the exponent should reflect on at its different levels of application: (1) purely as a response to a physical attack already launched, a countertactic; (2) as a response to a physical attack being launched but not yet fully developed, a simultaneously blended but overriding action; and (3) as a response to an impending attack, literally, beating the foe to the punch. The discussion of the strict ethical code attached to silat should never be a purely academic exercise, because silat techniques can quite easily kill the person against whom they are used. The orthodox ethical outlook of a genuine silat exponent rests in the sincere wish not to kill an assailant but simply to reduce his advantage while at the same time protecting himself from injury or death. If in the process, however, the attacker's life is lost, this regrettable circumstance is not glorified; the unfortunate victim is instead given due respect and, under certain circumstances, may even be honored.

2 BACKGROUND OF SILAT PERISAI DIRI

ORIGIN

Throughout Java, especially in its central and eastern regions and on the neighboring island of Bali, there is found a Malay system of combat called Silat Perisai Diri. The significance of this formal name is two-fold. Primary is that its founder and exponents regard their system as a wholly combative art that is neither recreational nor sportive. The combative nature of Silat Perisai Diri is evinced by the use of the word *silat*, which implies the application of systematic fighting techniques, in preference to the expression *penjak-silat*, which suggests artful physical action not necessarily intended for combat. Secondly, the formal name connotes a system of personal defense: *perisai*, meaning "shield," and *diri*, relating to one's "self." The shield, recognized in Indonesian culture as a weapon of self-defense, retains its significance as a symbol of both struggle and protection for the members of Silat Perisai Diri. Silat Perisai Diri is popularly referred to, for the sake of convenience, as P.D., by which initials it is well known across the length and breadth of Java.

P.D. is a modern system that is a synthesis of both combative rationale and techniques that stem from the remote past. The earliest efforts to formulate the P.D. system began in 1955 in Jogjakarta, central Java. But it was only with the inspiration and leadership of R.M.S. Dirdjoatmodjo of Surabaya, east Java, that the P.D. system emerged as an organized combative art. In the almost three decades in which Dirdjoatmodjo has been studying and teaching P.D., the system has finally evolved into a well-developed and highly respected art of self-defense. Today P.D. is practiced by almost 75,000 exponents throughout Indonesia and has international devotees in The Netherlands, France, Italy, Canada, the United States of America, and Australia. In addition to its mission of imparting practical knowledge of self-defense to persons in civilian life, P.D. is also taught to Indonesian army, navy, and special law-enforcement personnel; this attests to the highly practical and versatile nature of the system.

P.D. is, according to its founder, Dirdjoatmodjo, *silat asli* Melayu, that is, native or original silat in the sense of being a Malay-Muslim art of self-defense. Dirdjoatmodjo admits that P.D. is an eclectic system that combines different methods of combat selected from various ethno-cultural sources which have influenced the development of Indonesian culture since at least as early as the seventh century A.D. It is only natural that a man such as Dirdjoatmodjo, who has been vitally interested in weapons and combative arts all of his life, should acquire a wide range of experience and skill in combative arts. P.D., however, is and remains indisputably Malay in nature.

TECHNICAL RATIONALE

The technical base on which P.D. rests consists of a wide range of animal or animallike postures and movements, plus several that are typical of specially gifted human beings. Animal mannerisms have been adopted by P.D. because they enlarge upon human actions, thus bringing to them a wider range of self-defense applications. This combination of animal and human responses and actions gives P.D. no special claim to being unique inasmuch as many systems of combat found throughout Asia use identical technical bases. But the adoption of human and animal postures and movements into the P.D. system has been subject to modification by that most uncompromising factor in all history: the actions of man, who knows no law greater than the needs of his own existence. As a result, P.D. has developed a form of combat that has characteristics found in no other art.

One of these characteristics is that the P.D. adept will meet his assailant's attack with a bewildering sequence of posture changes and displacements that make liberal use of both linear and rotary actions applied, out of preference, from upright postures. All displacement movements are highly staccato in nature, and there is an easily discernable and unforgettable rhythmic, pulselike flow of action as the exponent moves and changes postures. All action is lightly made, is highly evasive, and occurs at an optimum rate of speed. P.D. is, therefore, an ideal system of self-defense for the person of average stature and build and is especially useful to one who prefers to avoid the brutally destructive forces that are generally the result of direct contact with a heavier, stronger, and more powerful assailant.

Sometimes, when faced with an enemy, the P.D. exponent will strike a dynamic pose. Avoiding eye contact with his foe, he fixes his gaze on the attacker's body, which appears as an inverted triangle with its vertex at the groin, and concentrates his attention by focusing on the solar plexus. More often than not, however, the P.D. exponent appears to the foe to be casual and almost indifferent to the presence of an enemy. He may look away, turn his body partially or wholly around, and present his back to the enemy as if to ignore the danger of the threat being posed to him. All of such actions by the P.D. exponent are but bait being held out to the unsuspecting enemy. Should the enemy accept what appears to him to be a splendid chance to launch his attack—an apparent weakness in the P.D. exponent's defense—he usually finds to his great dismay that he has been cleverly tricked; it is then too late to rectify such a mistake in judgment. A miscalculation of this sort can prove fatal.

The *jurus* (fundamentals) lie at the base of all training efforts in P.D. These fundamentals are arranged on a first-things-first basis in the order of learning and instruct the trainee in efficient applications of stance and postures and of displacement movements. At the same time they encourage the development of his body in the areas of functional strength and flexibility. Diligent practice of the fundamentals is the only way to mastery of the P.D. art of defense. A casual attitude toward training must be shunned.

In addition to learning the individual postures and the manner of moving from one posture to the appropriate next one, the trainee must learn to use the natural anatomical weapons of his body. He practices the individual techniques of punching, striking, blocking, parrying, and covering with his arms and hands; of kicking, kneeing, blocking, and parrying with his legs, knees, and feet; of butting with his head, shoulders, and buttocks. All training is conducted on the basis of drills made in solo fashion or with the aid of a training partner; the latter kind of drill is carefully controlled by the method called *rahsia* (secrets), which corresponds to training exercises that are carefully controlled in order to avoid serious injury or death.

Silat P.D. is not purely an unarmed approach to self-defense. All genuine Malay silat systems acknowledge the importance and need for weapons in the defense of one's person. It is highly idealistic and ridiculously foolish to expect to enter combat and emerge unharmed by depending only on empty-hand skills. Nor is the assumption that at times one is unarmed, that one does not always carry a weapon, a valid justification for neglecting the study of weaponry. That the well-trained exponent of silat is *never* unarmed under any condition is an accepted adage among silat exponents in all styles.

The P.D. exponent can effectively make use of almost any object as a weapon, be it a stone, branch, or domestically useful instrument like a comb, key, pencil, or book. But his normal training regimen centers on the use of a variety of instruments that are primarily intended to be used as weapons. These include as standard weapons the *pisau* (a nondescript knife), the *parang* (a chopper-cleaver type of long knife), the *keris* (the Malay national weapon featuring a double cutting-edge in various forms), the *pedang* (sword), the *bessi tjabang* (a metal truncheon with two tine projections that emerge at the junction of the shaft and handle), and the *toya* (a length of wood in the form of a stick or staff). More specialized weapons also characterize the P.D. arsenal: the *arbir* (a single-cutting-edged halberd), the *tekken* (a short length of cane featuring a hooked handle), and the *roti kalong* (a metal "knuckle-duster").

The P.D. exponent seeks to develop six personal attributes or qualities:

1. maximum technical precision
2. optimum speed in reflex action
3. unfailing reaction appropriate to any emergency situation
4. maximum physical strength
5. enduring patience
6. everlasting tranquillity

The above order of achievement corresponds to the different levels of the trainee's expertise in silat, to the degree of his all-around finesse in the art. These levels of progress range at the onset from purely physical motor skills to the much more important spiritual values of which more must now be said.

SPIRITUAL RATIONALE

In his technical development and consequently evolving spiritual maturity, the P.D. trainee proceeds with fervent dedication to training methods that build "outer strength," that is, physical stamina and power in the application of techniques intended to preserve him from whatever physical harm may be intended by an assailant. Through a protracted period of study and training in basic motor skills the exponent may hope to excel in the art of self-defense. With such expertise he stands at the threshold of the development of his "inner power," the spiritual reservoir of strength that indelibly marks him and secures for him the position of a *guru* (teacher) of the P.D. system. With a sufficient display of inner power he may even rise to the exhalted position of the *maha guru* (master-teacher). From this, the summit of the mastery of silat technique, he may then eventually emerge as a *pandekar* (spiritualist and master-teacher), the paragon of spirituality in silat circles.

The pandekar possesses the ability to heal injury and sickness through the medium of prayer and can invoke the necessary combinations of the spiritual strengths of charms, incantations, and omens in order to negate the influences of evil acting upon those persons who have dedicated themselves to the teachings of a pandekar. There are some people, especially in the Western world, who scoff at such claims, but Dirdjoatmodjo is a recognized pandekar whose spiritual powers have been demonstrated on many occasions in the presence of credible witnesses.

As the P.D. exponent gains skill with physical motor skills he must learn the method of *gwakang* (breathing) if he is to attain spiritual insight and capabilities. This method of breath control not only strengthens muscular actions but is also related to meditational aspects of P.D. training that, in turn, lie at the base of *lima bokok,* the "five centers of spirituality." Knowledge of these centers is attainable only by members of P.D. who have devoted a lifetime to the study of the art. The spiritual centers are symbolically represented by the official P.D. emblem, which is in the form of a pentagon.

Perhaps the best way the trainee can prepare himself to understand the spiritual nature of P.D. is to realize that P.D. is a Muslim art of self-defense and that its values and tenets are based on the Islamic religious code. The question may arise rather naturally as to whether or not the exponent of P.D. must subscribe to the Islamic faith. Perhaps the best answer to this is simply, "It would be best." But pandekar Dirdjoatmodjo shows great tolerance and wisdom in permitting non-Muslim candidates for study of P.D. to retain whatever religious beliefs they may have. This position has, of course, earned both Dirdjoatmodjo and the P.D. system criticism from some orthodox Muslims. Yet the non-Muslim world is much richer for the tolerant stand being taken by Dirdjoatmodjo, and perhaps there will be a greater understanding of, if not conversion to, the Islamic faith than would be possible without his teachings.

Islamic prayer, *do'a,* plays an important role in all P.D. training routines. Prayer is a matter for the individual exponent's attention and indicates his respect for and adherence to Islamic doctrine. A religious state of mind must pervade all training in P.D. and its applications. Without the tempering effect of religious values no system of self-defense can rise above sheer acts of rowdy violence. In order to develop an awareness of the importance of religious values in P.D. exponents, Dirdjoatmodjo has structured P.D. *hormat* (customary formal etiquette) in prayer form. Whether training alone or with a partner or partners, every exponent of P.D. is expected to render the hormat in a sincere and pious frame of mind. The hormat symbolizes awareness of the great things that flow from Allah (God) above down to earth and so to the everlasting benefit of grateful man. It is also a method by which one shows respect to fellow human beings.

RENDERING THE HORMAT

Once at the commencement of training and once again at the conclusion of training the trainee renders the hormat. The following should be used as a guide to its proper execution. Boldface numbers after black diamonds indicate the photos that correspond to the text explanations.

1

2

3

4

5

6

Solo Method

◆1. Stand erect with your feet positioned slightly apart; allow your arms to hang naturally at your sides. Keep your eyes open and focus them to your front as if looking at the horizon. Relax all tension in your body and pause momentarily as you breathe at a normal rate of inhalation and expiration.

◆2. Reach up and slowly extend your arms to their full limit overhead; position your hands with the palms facing, but not touching, each other. As you raise your arms, follow with your eyes the upward movement of your hands, finally to gaze beyond their extended position into space. Pause momentarily.

◆3, 4. Slowly bend your arms and bring your hands downward in a vertical line of descent in front of your body; allow your left hand to slightly precede your right hand. Follow the descent of your hands with your eyes.

◆5. Continue to lower your hands and once again bring them into a palms-opposing position as you stop their descent at the level of your heart. Focus your eyes to the front as if looking at the horizon. Pause momentarily.

◆6. Slowly lower and separate your hands as you bring your arms alongside your body to the natural position in which you began.

1

2

3

4

5

Partner Method

When executing the hormat with a training partner each exponent should do exactly as he did for solo training, but he must now synchronize his movements with those of his partner. But if the student is training with a recognized teacher of the P.D. system there are some minor differences as follows.

◆1. The teacher (right) raises and extends his arms to a position overhead that is higher than that assumed by the student. The student positions his palms facing forward and points them slightly upward facing his teacher's hands; he concentrates his gaze on his teacher's hands.

◆2. Both teacher and student slowly lower their hands at the same rate of descent, the left hand preceding the right hand; the student's hands travel a shorter distance.

◆3. When the teacher and student have positioned their hands at the level of their hearts, they mutually pause and let their eyes meet.

◆4. Maintaining eye contact, the teacher begins to lower his arms to his sides; he is followed by the student, who does similarly.

◆5. Teacher and student terminate the hormat by standing erect with their arms alongside their bodies. They maintain eye contact with each other.

3 STANCES AND POSTURES

ABOUT SIKAP

One important fundamental of effective P.D. technique lies in the exponent's choice and use of *sikap asli*. *Sikap* is a Malay word which, for the P.D. exponent, refers not only to his physical carriage or bearing—his way of standing and moving—but also to his mental bearing, his way of thinking, feeling, and behaving. The term *asli* is used here in the sense of "original," as has already been explained. Thus, sikap are composite attitudes of mind and body that make reference to different combinations of stance and posture as they apply to combative ardor.

Stance refers to the position of the exponent's lower body, primarily his legs. In P.D., extremely wide stances are given very limited application. It is true that wide stances generally increase the user's stability; but they also adversely affect his mobility. The P.D. system depends for its effect on fast, lightly made evasive movements, which cannot be made when a wide-legged stance is used. For that reason, the P.D. exponent prefers to use what he calls a "natural" stance in which his feet are positioned about the distance between his shoulders apart.

Posture refers to the exponent's overall body position, particularly that of his upper torso areas, arms, and head. The relationship between stance and posture is obvious, but it should be understood that one can assume various different stances while maintaining the same posture; the opposite is also true. Thus for any one single sikap there will be some variations possible in the combination of stance and posture; additionally, sikap have both right and left derivatives. P.D. exponents prefer the erect or upright natural posture since it strongly complements the natural stance. Together, the natural stance and natural posture permit the greatest mobility, speed, and, consequently, the maximum possible evasive movement.

P.D. technique, based on the natural stance and natural posture in various forms, has been scientifically studied and designed to produce the greatest economy of energy in the generation of force used to deal effectively with an assailant. But P.D., in comparison with many other Asian combative arts, can still be described as a loose system. It does not make ironclad specifications in regard to distances between the feet, angles of delivery, or other aspects of technique. Thus, a stance that feels natural to an exponent is for him a natural stance. Other modifications of basic stances and postures will arise owing to actual combat conditions. The trainee should keep these points in mind when practicing the sikap introduced here and when studying and performing the training exercises presented in chapter 5.

In the preceding chapter it was stated that the P.D. system uses the peculiarities of both animal and human actions in the formulation of its self-defense techniques. Three sikap are based on human mannerisms, while seven are based on the mannerisms of animals or animallike creatures. These ten sikap are as follows.

Sikap Based on Human Mannerisms

1. *pendeta,* the priest
2. *putri,* the princess
3. *setria,* the patriot

Sikap Based on Animal Mannerisms

1. *burung kuntul,* the crane
2. *garuda,* the golden eagle
3. *harimau,* the tiger
4. *kuda kuningang,* the brass horse
5. *lingsang,* the otter
6. *melewis,* the swallow
7. *naga,* the dragonlike animal

Various forms of sikap putri

Sikap pendeta

THE HUMAN SIKAP

The Malay word *pendeta* refers to a scholar, a learned person, and is typified in the person of the priest or clergyman. This dynamic positional attitude, *sikap pendeta,* depicts steadfast character, unwavering discipline, and wisdom in dealing with crises. To assume this sikap, center your weight over both legs, then turn your lead foot so that the toes point a bit inward. Form two clenched fists, knuckles down (the formation of the silat fist is explained on page 29) ; the arm on the side of your retreated leg should be held close to your body. (Here and elsewhere, detail photos and views from different angles are provided to help the trainee's understanding of positions and techniques.)

Sikap putri depicts the typical princess, a daughter of royalty. It displays a refined elegance and stately dignity such as would accompany a princess engaged in various domestic situations (waiting on guests, dressing, worshiping). It takes various forms—known by names like *sikap bunga* or *sikap putri berhias*—but all are predominately back stances. Distribute your body-weight on a 60–40 basis favoring your retreated leg. Use only the open-hand palm formations of both hands (p. 32) when you assume this sikap.

Various forms of sikap setria

In *sikap setria,* the patriot, are depicted the qualities of steadfast loyalty, true and faithful obedience to a recognized superior being or cause. This sikap, too, takes several forms. Characteristic of this sikap is the use of two clenched fists, one of which must be held, arm bent, high overhead, the other, arm bent, across the body at the level of the belt. Distribute your weight on a 60–40 basis over your retreated or lead leg as is appropriate.

Sikap burung kuntul

Sikap garuda

Sikap harimau

THE ANIMAL SIKAP

The crane, a huge bird, gives the basic inspiration for *sikap burung kuntul.* This sikap depicts the crane as it stands on one leg; it is defending its own sphere, but at the same time it is in readiness for instant counterattack against unwanted aggression. Stand on one leg; raise the other leg, bend it at the knee, and turn its outer thigh area toward the enemy. Form and use the semi-clenched fist (p. 30) with this sikap.

Sikap garuda represents a mythological creature, the golden eagle of the Indonesian national coat of arms. This bird symbolizes creative energy; its principal color (gold) suggests the greatness of the Indonesian nation, while its secondary color (black) represents nature. This sikap requires that you raise both arms on an upward diagonal in front of you; stretch out the arm on the side of your advanced leg and hold the other arm somewhat close to your body. Hold both hands in claw-hand formation (p. 31), palms facing forward. Distribute your bodyweight on a 60–40 basis favoring your leading leg.

Sikap harimau depicts the tiger, a beast well known for its cunning and ferocity. In assuming this sikap do not confuse it with *sikap garuda,* which it resembles. Stretch out both your arms on an upward diagonal in front of you. Hold both hands in claw-hand formation, palms facing downward. Distribute your bodyweight on a 60–40 basis favoring your leading leg.

The acrobatic action of the swallow in rapid flight, its limitless number of movements as it soars and glides gracefully through the air, is represented by *sikap melewis.* Hold both hands in

Sikap melewis

Sikap naga

beak-hand formation (p. 31) and assume a back-stance so that your retreated leg receives about 70 percent of your bodyweight.

Another mythological creature is the *naga,* a dragonlike animal that resembles the crocodile and the snake; it is believed to have claws and to be capable of breathing out blasts of fire. The special characteristic of *sikap naga* is that one arm is raised high overhead, fully outstretched, while the other is outstretched downward in front of the body. Hold both hands in palm-hand formation and distribute your bodyweight on a 60–40 basis in favor of your retreated leg; position your feet somewhat closer together than is the case for the other sikap.

Two sikap are not illustrated here since they are not needed to execute the techniques presented in this book. These are *sikap lingsang,* which represents the lithe and quick body of the otter, and *sikap kuda kuningang,* the sturdy-legged position taken by a brass statue of a horse.

You will learn how to apply the different sikap in connection with the training exercises described in chapter 5. But you should practice the sikap themselves before undertaking those exercises. Learn to move quickly and directly into the sikap from a normal posture while standing or moving. It is also recommended that you learn to move from one sikap to another in succession and in different orders of occurrence. A large wall mirror will help you spot any errors in your sikap. Once you have workable familiarity with the different sikap and can assume them without thinking about what you are doing, go on to the training exercises.

4 WEAPONS AND VITAL AREAS

The human body has many inherent weaknesses. In formulating systems and techniques of combat the trained fighting man makes a careful and detailed study of how to protect as well as how to exploit these anatomical weaknesses. He notes the origins and insert areas of muscles, ligaments, and tendons; the places of articulation of the joints; nerve centers; veins and arteries; and other places on the human body that will likely produce acute pain or loss of consciousness when properly struck. Since man's vital anatomical weaknesses are the targets of combative techniques, there is an intrinsic relationship between these vital areas and the way in which weapons are used.

The P.D. exponent makes use of both anatomical and instrumental weapons. When he accurately impacts either kind of weapon against an enemy's vital areas, he naturally expects to obtain the submission of the foe. His choice of a vital target area, however, depends primarily on what effect he is looking for. A trained exponent can choose to discourage the enemy from making further aggressive moves, to stun and immobilize him, to render him unconscious, or to deal him a crippling or lethal blow.

But at times the exponent's choice is severely conditioned by the factors of terrain and climate, or by the manner in which the foe conducts his attack. Any one of these things, as well as any of them in combination with the others, can serve either to enhance or to negate the effects of a self-defense response. Consider the following cases.

Features of the terrain can work powerful effects on either the attacker or defender, and the technique of making the best use of terrain can gain for one an advantage over the other. The attacker will have an advantage if he plans and executes his attack in terrain that restricts the defender's avenues of movement or that gives insecure footing and thus limits his victim's choice of response. The intended victim, however, must strive to overcome his disadvantage by using techniques that are effective under conditions of minimum stability and movement. Important in his selection of technique is his need to improve the effect of his response by acting in harmony with the forces of gravity. The use of leg and foot tactics, for example, is less likely to be successful than is the use of the arms and hands; and throwing an attacker forward uphill is much more difficult than throwing him in a downhill direction.

Warm climate can directly aid the application of technique, for the combatants will usually be lightly clad, with more vital areas exposed than would be if they clashed in colder climates. Heavy clothing can conceal or otherwise substantially protect vital areas, and many techniques are rendered ineffective because of such clothing. The wearing of bulky clothing, too, hinders the wearer's ability to maneuver quickly and easily.

A foe who launches his attack by direct or announced confrontation with his intended victim may be much easier to deal with than the crafty foe who chooses the sneaky tactic of ambush. Here the element of surprise is being exploited to the utmost by the attacker, and this greatly enhances his chances for success. But the defender must seek to offset both the physical and psychological advantage gained by the foe who strikes from ambush by incorporating the element of surprise into his own response. He may be able to do so only if he is sufficiently trained to the point where he recognizes beforehand the possible dangers in the areas through which he must pass, those places whose terrain and other factors may conceal to the last instant a lurking foe. The defender must be trained to be aware at all times of the conditions that surround him and of their possible danger to him.

The foregoing summary indicates the importance of the degree to which the defender is trained in the handling of self-defense situations. It is vital to the physical and psychological development of the P.D. exponent to learn how to make the best use of the situation, no matter what disadvantage it presents to him at the time of the emergency. All training in P.D. is directed toward this goal. For this reason the P.D. training program is always conducted under a variety of realistic conditions, any of which might prevail when the enemy strikes. Training is conducted both in and out of doors and gives the exponent a wide range of experiences that would not be possible were training carried out solely under ideal conditions or on a level and matted gymnasium floor. The P.D. training session, therefore, not only is directed toward the development of good techniques, but also is intended to be a severe challenge to the exponent's ability to instantly adapt himself to different and difficult situations. P.D. training methods stand the exponent in good stead by promoting his sense of self-confidence. Should a self-defense emergency arise he knows that his chances for dealing successfully with it are optimum.

Because of the innate relationship between the use of weapons and vital anatomical weaknesses it is characteristic of basic P.D. training programs to combine the study of anatomical weapons with that of the targets on the human body they are best directed against. For convenience this combined study can be divided into several categories, formations using (1) the single hand, (2) the single arm, (3) the shoulder, (4) the head, (5) two hands, and (6) the feet and legs. We shall examine each of these categories in the remaining pages of this chapter, but some brief comments will be useful here.

Trainees are advised that the suggested targets for the different formations of anatomical weapons are stated largely with the understanding that the operator is on his feet as he deals with a foe who is in a relatively similar stance and posture, and that he may be positioned in front of, at the sides of, or behind the foe. The introduction of other positional attitudes may possibly expand, reduce, or otherwise modify the suggested methods of delivery of the anatomical weapons as well as their target areas. This may be the case when, for example, the foe is bent over, or when either the defender or his aggressor, or both, are kneeling or are in a supine or prone position on the ground. Though these situations are not specifically explained and illustrated in this chapter, several examples do appear in the training exercises in chapter 5. They should not prove troublesome to the exponent who has mastered the fundamentals given here.

All trainees in the P.D. system must constantly bear in mind that Silat P.D. is not a sport—a game to be played in sport-competition style. The system is an effective means of defense and all of its techniques present danger to the person who receives them.

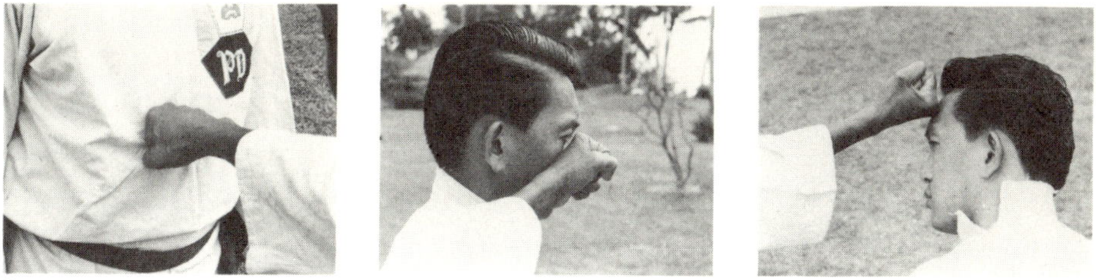

Clenched fist: thrust-punch, backhand strike, hammer-blow

USE OF THE SINGLE HAND

A P.D. exponent knows many applications for the use of a single hand as a weapon. With the hand he is able to deliver powerful striking, punching, and other actions. The most basic of these actions involve three types of hand formations: (1) the clenched fist, (2) the semiclenched fist, and (3) the open hand.

The Clenched Fist

Form a fist in the usual way, bending and curling your four fingers tightly into your palm; bend and press your thumb tightly against your forefinger and middle finger to seal the fist.

Deliver your clenched fist straight forward in a thrust-punch so that the back of your hand is uppermost at the instant the fist strikes the target. Use the area on the fist that lies between the base and mid-knuckles of your curled fingers as a contact surface against these targets: mid-body areas (solar plexus, heart, liver, ribs, kidneys, spine): lower-body areas (groin).

Use your clenched fist in a backhand strike, delivering it laterally or diagonally, upward or downward, across the front of your body so that the outer surface of that fist, from the wrist to the base knuckles of the fingers, is the part that strikes against the following recommended targets: facial areas (mouth, nose, eyes, cheekbones, chin); head areas (temples, ears, base of the skull); sides of the neck; mid-body areas (solar plexus, heart, ribs, liver, kidneys); lower-body areas (groin). Use your clenched fist in a vertical or diagonal downward hammer-blow with only the base knuckles of the fist acting as the contact surface. Strike against any of the following recommended vital areas: facial areas (mouth, nose, eyes, cheekbones); head areas (temples, ears, forehead); sides of the neck; the upper arms, forearms, or backs of the hands of the foe's extended arms; the thigh muscles, shins, or insteps of the foe's extended legs.

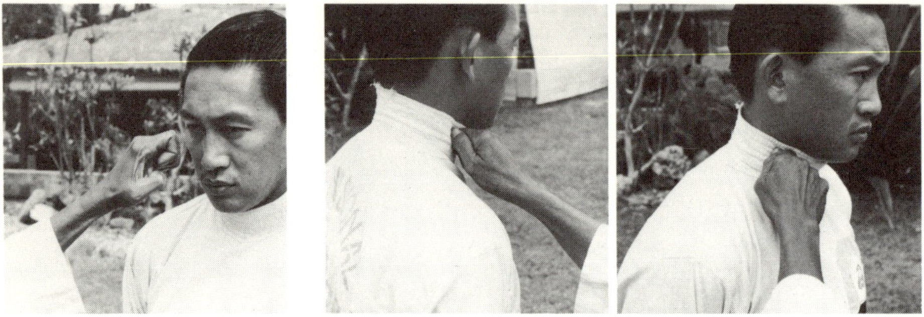

Semiclenched fist: thrust-punch and arrowhead fist

The Semiclenched Fist

Relax the tension in your tightly clenched fist and allow your fingers to uncurl just a little bit; but keep them touching each other. Bend your thumb as you did when making the clenched fist, but do not press it up against your fingers; it stands alone. Deliver the semiclenched fist in a forward thrust-punch so that the back of your hand is uppermost at the instant the fist impacts against the target. Use only the mid-knuckles of your four fingers as the contact surface against these recommended targets: facial areas (mouth, nose, eyes, chin, cheekbones); head areas (temples, ears, base of the skull); throat; sides of the neck; mid-body areas (solar plexus, sternum, pectoral muscles, ribs, heart, kidneys, liver, spine); lower-body areas (groin); the upper arms, forearms, or backs of the hands of the foe's extended arms; the thigh muscles, shins, or insteps of the foe's extended legs.

Reform a clenched fist but this time shape it a bit differently. Jut your forefinger and middle finger forward so that your hand roughly takes the shape of an arrowhead; the mid-knuckles of your forefinger and middle finger are its tip. Press your bent thumb against the forefinger to fix both of these digits in place. Thrust-punch this fist forward so that the back of your hand is uppermost as the fist impacts against the target; use the mid-knuckle of your forefinger as a contact surface against the following recommended targets: facial areas (eyes, mouth, nose, cheekbones); head areas (temples, ears); sides of the neck; throat; mid-body areas (solar plexus, ribs, sternum, pectoral muscles, kidneys, liver); lower-body areas (groin); the upper arms, forearms, or backs of the hands of the foe's extended arms; the thigh muscles, shins, or insteps of the foe's extended legs.

Beak-hand

Whip

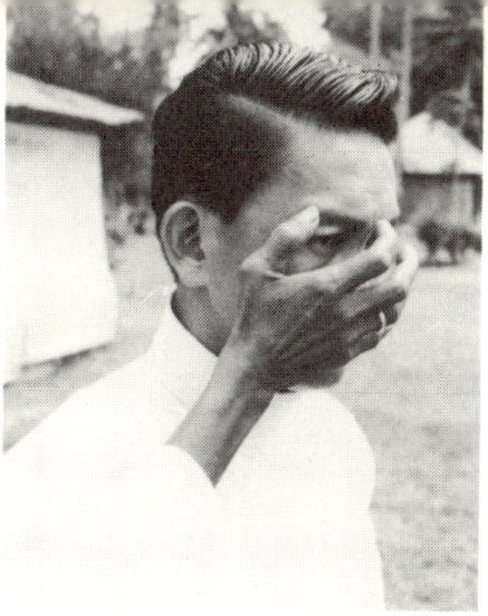
Claw-hand

The Open Hand

Basic use of the single open-hand formation includes applications of (a) the fingers, (b) the knife-edge, and (c) the palm.

FINGERS. The P.D. exponent uses his fingers with powerful effect in different ways by simulating either the actions of a bird beak, a whip, or an animal claw.

To form the *beak-hand,* bring the tips of your fingers and the thumb of one hand together and compress them into the smallest possible area. Use birdlike pecks or strikes to deliver the combined tips of your fingers and thumb as a single contact surface against these recommended targets: facial areas (eyes, nose, mouth); head areas (temples, ears); throat; sides of the neck.

The effective use of your fingers as a *whip* depends on your ability to completely relax your wrist and fingers. Open your hand and allow your fingers and the thumb to spread apart. Deliver this relatively limp formation of the hand in a backhand strike that moves laterally or diagonally, upward or downward, across the front of your body as if you were cracking a whip; the back surface of your hand up to the tips of your fingers should be the part that impacts against these recommended targets: facial areas (eyes, mouth, nose, cheekbones); head areas (ears, temples); sides of the neck; throat.

The *claw-hand* resembles an animal paw with its claws extended or a birdlike talon. Make it by spreading and curling the ends of your fingers, taking care not to overbend the mid-knuckles of your hand; bend and position your thumb so that it is not touching your fingers. Use this hand formation in a raking or tearing action, with the tips of your fingers (the fingernails as well) as a contact surface against these vital areas: facial areas (eyes, mouth, cheeks); head areas (ears); sides of the neck; throat.

KNIFE-EDGE. With the knife-edge of your hand use as a contact surface only the region on the little-finger side that lies between the base of the little finger and the heelbone of the hand where it

Knife-edge: backhand, lateral, diagonal blows

Palm-hand

joins the wrist. Extend and hold the fingers of one hand together but allow your thumb to stand away from the forefinger; keep tension throughout the hand. A wide range of deliveries is possible with this hand formation. Strike lateral or diagonal blows, upward or downward, in backhand fashion across the front of your body, holding the back of your hand uppermost; strike lateral or diagonal blows, upward or downward, across the front of your body with the palm up; strike blows straight down ahead of you; strike vertical rising blows back behind you. Use the following targets: facial areas (nose, mouth, cheekbones, eyes); head areas (temples, ears, base of the skull); sides of the neck; throat; clavicles; mid-body areas (ribs, kidneys, heart, solar plexus); lower-body areas (groin); the upper arms, forearms, or backs of the hands of the foe's extended arms; the thigh muscles or shins of the foe's extended legs.

PALM-HAND. Form the palm-hand by holding one hand open, the fingers extended and not spread apart, with the tips of the fingers slightly curled; straighten your thumb and position it so that it touches the inner surface on the edge of the base knuckle of your forefinger. Keep moderate tension throughout the hand so that the hand, when upturned, resembles a shallow tray. Deliver the palm-hand and use the lower area of the palm near the heel of the hand to strike against the target. Two basic deliveries of the palm-hand are the jab and the roundhouse loop.

Jab your palm-hand in a lateral, rising, or descending trajectory against these targets: facial areas (chin, nose, cheekbones); head areas (temples, ears, base of the skull); mid-body areas (sternum, solar plexus, ribs); lower-body areas (groin, buttocks).

Deliver a roundhouse loop with the palm-hand by swinging it laterally or in a rising or descending trajectory across the front of your body to cup-impact against any of these recommended areas: facial areas (mouth, eyes, nose); head areas (ears); mid-body areas (solar plexus); lower-body areas (groin).

Wrist

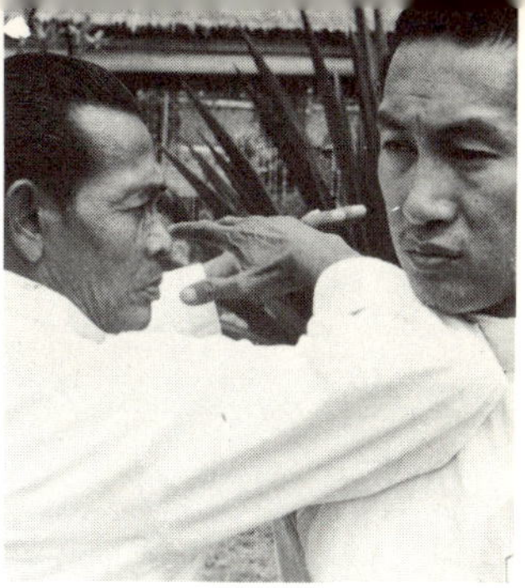

Forearm-elbow: driving action

USE OF THE SINGLE ARM

The P.D. exponent makes powerful use of his arms to strike an assailant. The basic uses of the arm involve: (1) the wrist and (2) the forearm-elbow.

The Wrist

A flexed wrist presents one of the hardest surfaces found on the human body. Open your hand and flex your wrist by straightening and bringing your fingers and thumb together, curving the upper and back surface of your wrist in a convex manner; keep a moderate degree of tension in your hand to give unity to this formation.

Maintain this curved formation of your wrist when you strike in backhand fashion with either a straight, lateral, or diagonal rising action against the aggressor; use the area on the back of your wrist where the hand and arm join together to make contact with the following recommended vital areas: facial areas (chin, nose, mouth, eyes, cheekbones); head areas (temples, ears); mid-body areas (solar plexus, ribs); lower-body areas (groin).

The Forearm-Elbow

The use of the forearm-elbow in close-quarter combat is a specialty of the P.D. exponent. The formation of this anatomical weapon is simple, and there are various manners of applying it. Merely bend your arm at the elbow and make use of the outer surface of your arm from just above the wrist to the tip of your elbow.

Deliver the forearm-elbow in a driving action in front of you, directing it against these recommended vital areas: facial areas (chin, mouth, nose, cheekbones); head areas (temples, ears, base

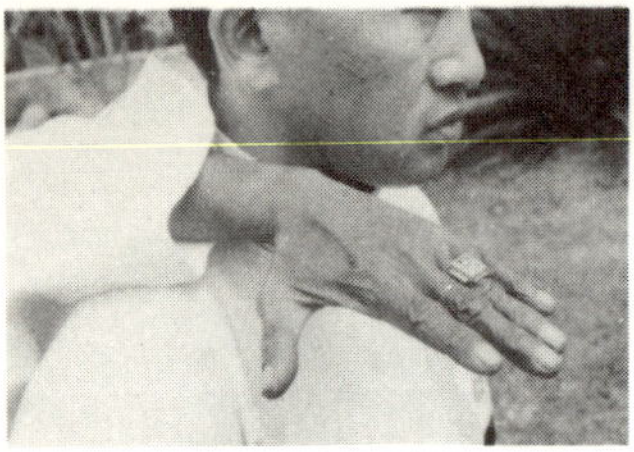

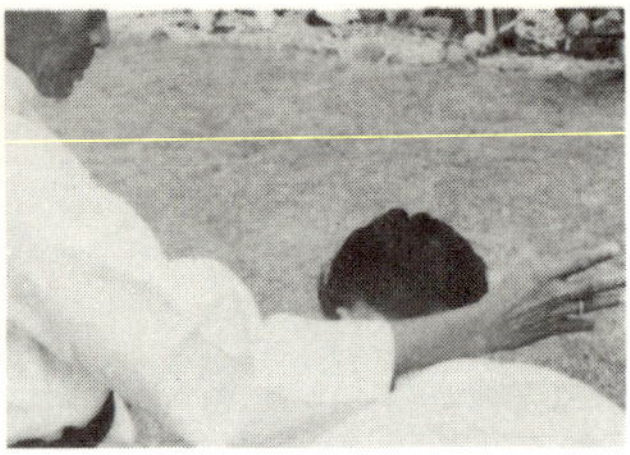

Forearm-elbow: backhand and vertical chops

Shoulder

of the skull) ; sides of the neck; throat; mid-body areas (sternum, ribs).

A backhand chop is also possible with the forearm-elbow. Deliver it much as you would when using the knife-edge of your hand, but change the contact surface. These targets are recommended: facial areas (chin, nose, mouth, cheekbones) ; head areas (temples, ears, base of the skull) ; sides of the neck; throat; mid-body areas (sternum, ribs).

A vertical downward chop made to your front is another basic use of the forearm-elbow. The part of your arm that makes contact is the same as in the previous two examples. Strike downward against these targets: exposed facial or head areas.

USE OF THE SHOULDER

That the shoulder can be an effective weapon may not seem possible at first glance, but the P.D. exponent makes good use of it. He uses it in push-shove and butting actions against an attacker, more to set the foe up for further and more decisive action to follow than to inflict heavy punishment on him. The side and top surfaces of the shoulder are used against these targets: mid-body areas (sternum, solar plexus, ribs, spine) ; lower-body areas (thighs, buttocks).

When using the shoulder against an enemy it is wise to form and ready both hands as clenched fists. Position the fist on the side of the shoulder you will use near your upper thigh on the same side; position the fist of your free arm near the biceps of the arm whose shoulder will be employed. Both fists held in this way not only serve to cover your vital areas but are ready for the follow-up action that must accompany the shoulder's push-shove or butting tactics.

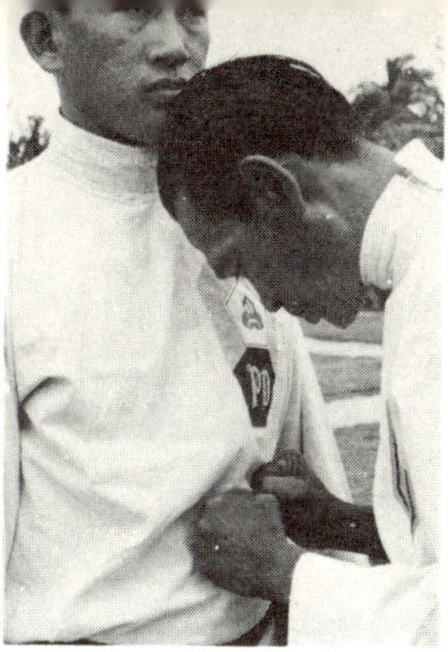
Head

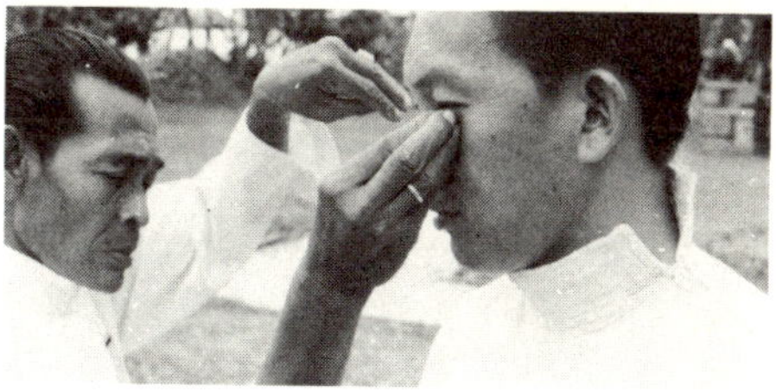
Double eye-jab

USE OF THE HEAD

Some judicious use of the head can be made in close-quarter combat, but this must not be overdone. The P.D. exponent uses his head as a weapon to butt the enemy, making contact with the front part of the forehead and the upper dome region of the head against these recommended targets: facial areas (chin, nose, cheekbones); head areas (temples, ears, base of the skull); lower-body areas (groin). The hands are used to protect the solar plexus and the groin.

USE OF TWO HANDS

The P.D. system uses a wide variety of double-hand formations and tactics to subdue an enemy. Only the most basic of these methods will be considered here. These are all directed against facial areas because these areas are very vulnerable and difficult to protect. The trainee is advised at this point to restudy the use of the single-hand formations with more than just a little care; these simpler methods lie at the root of effective use of two hands.

That the double-hand tactics are drastic measures which are particularly dangerous should be obvious. These tactics must be practiced with extreme care in order to avoid needless injury. Moreover, they must be used only in the most desperate of circumstances and then only when there is absolutely no other recourse. Any of the P.D. two-hand methods shown here can produce death through internal damage to the brain and cervical region of the spine.

The Double Eye-Jab

Make a beak-hand with each of your hands. Use both beak-hands to jab or peck like a bird into your assailant's eyes. When you strike you may do so with both hands simultaneously or alternately. Striking continuously is usually unnecessary.

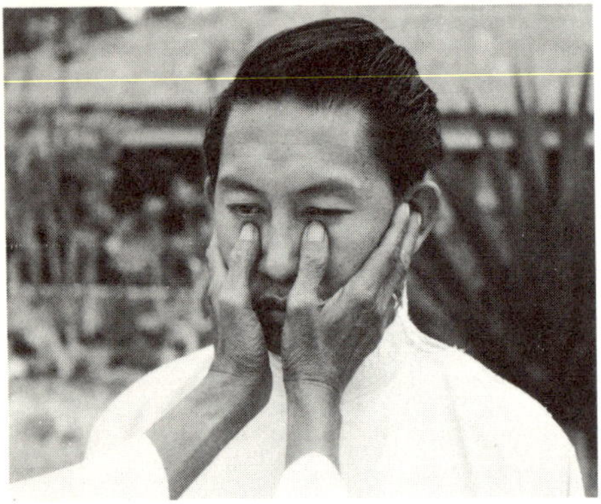

Double eye-gouge

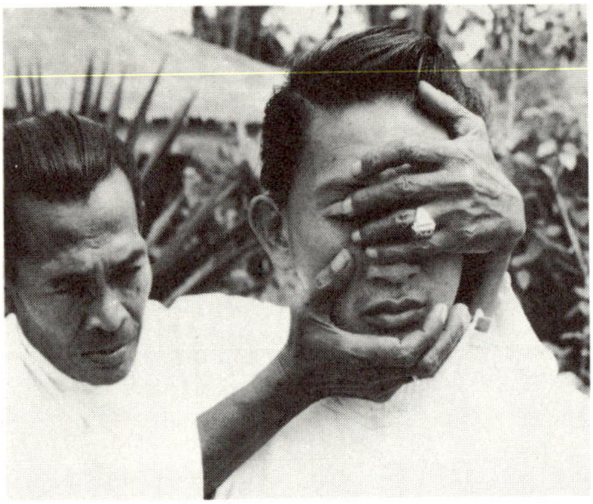

Eye tear and neck twist

The Double Eye-Gouge

Open both of your hands; straighten and separate all digits. Position both hands with the palms facing, heels of the hands somewhat closer together than the fingertips, in front of you at the level of your solar plexus. Use both hands in an upward driving thrust to initiate the double eye-gouge. Thrust both hands upward and forward against the assailant's face. The heels of your palms should be directed to strike against the assailant's chin; at the very instant that you make this contact hold his head in both hands with your fingers extended upward along the sides of his cheeks. The force of this initial blow will snap his head backward, and this is usually enough to make him submit. But if appropriate, while maintaining contact with both of your palms on his face, slide your thumbs upward on each side of his nose and drive the tips of your thumbs squarely into his eyes.

The Eye Tear and Neck Twist

This tactic is applied from a position behind the assailant. It is generally used to bring the foe off-balance backward or to hurl him around and backward to the ground. The positions of the hands as they appear in the photograph may be reversed.

After you have maneuvered to a position behind your attacker, reach around his head and place one of your open hands over the front of his face, covering his eyes and most of his nose; this is your upper hand. Use your other open hand, the lower hand, to cup his chin from underneath, your thumb extending upward along one of his cheeks.

From this position of advantage you have several powerful options. By applying combined pressure with the fingers of your upper hand against the assailant's eyeballs and an upward and backward pull of your lower hand against his chin you can easily move his head backward. Almost any person will submit instantly under this treatment. Should more severe punishment be required, however, you can haul the assailant directly backward to the ground. Or you may swing him circularly around to either side as may be appropriate. A forceful snapping action made with your lower hand can easily break the assailant's neck; and the fingers of your upper hand can just as easily rip out one or both of his eyes.

USE OF THE FEET AND LEGS

All basic uses of the feet and legs in the P.D. system have one important thing in common. No tactic requires that the exponent bring his foot to a level higher than that of the enemy's solar plexus. The reasoning behind this has considerable merit.

Actual experience has shown that action taken in combat waged for one's life is considerably different from any action taken in sport-oriented forms of mock combat. Mock combat is, in any of its forms of "free practice" sparring or grappling (the so-called full-contact systems), only a game in the playful sense of the word. The participating individual in the sport-game always plays his part with the very comfortable psychological advantage of knowing that in spite of making mistakes, receiving rough handling, or proving himself to be inferior in skill, he will survive the clash with his opponent or opponents. He will most likely be able to try again should he fail.

The conduct of the sport-game is considered proper only when the participants display a sporting attitude, that is, when they "play fair" by adhering to rules that are always designed to make the participation interesting and as safe as possible. Not so in real combat where there are no rules and an "anything goes" attitude prevails. The opponent is an enemy, one who is determined and doing his best to injure or take the life of his victim. In real combat, for which the P.D. system is designed, there is no sane reason for deliberately giving the enemy any good (sporting) chance to attain victory.

Because of the lethal potential of real combat the P.D. exponent prefers to use his feet and legs in ways that do not overly expose him to counterattack. He knows that a kicking tactic is already based on a calculated risk; he must momentarily stand on one leg in a position that affords him minimal stability. Adding to this risk is the fact that a kick to an area lying high up on the foe's body takes more time to deliver than does a kick made to lower areas; the high kick travels over a longer distance. Thus, the high kicker, while he is in an imperfect state of balance, gives the foe more opportunity for counterattack. That any kick delivered to a high target is easier to anticipate, misdirect, or stop than a kick made to lower areas, is yet another important consideration.

Compounding the risk taken when one kicks at high targets is the factor of terrain discussed earlier in this chapter. So important is this factor that it is repeated here. High kicks, which inherently render the kicker unstable, do so even more when they are made on irregular, slippery, or otherwise unpredictable ground; and in some cases they are impossible to execute.

The P.D. exponent is trained to use his feet and legs to inflict direct punishment on the foe, but he also uses them to obstruct the attacker's movements. To accomplish these two important things the exponent uses various formations that involve use of (1) the ball, (2) the sole, (3) the instep, (4) the heel, (5) the outer anklebone, (6) the inner-edge and anklebone, (7) the shinbone, (8) the calf, and (9) the knee.

The Ball

The underportion of the foot just below the base of the toes, the ball, makes an effective weapon when it is delivered straight forward in a snap-kick or a roundhouse kick. In either case curl the toes of your foot upward; maintain tension throughout the upper part of your foot in order to keep your toes in the proper position and to expose the ball of your foot. Use the snap-kick and roundhouse kick to inflict direct injury on the foe by delivering these actions against the following recommended targets: midbody areas (solar plexus, ribs, liver, heart, kidneys, spine); lower-body areas (groin, front portion of the kneecap, inner thigh muscles at the knee).

To obstruct the foe's movements deliver the ball of your foot in snap-kick or roundhouse trajectories but with less force than would be needed to inflict direct injury. Direct these kicks to the front of the foe's kneecaps or against the inner surfaces of either knee.

PUNISHMENT

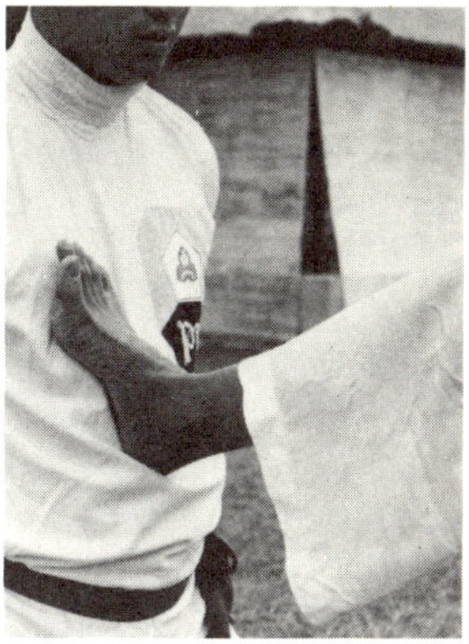

OBSTRUCTION

Ball: snap-kick

Ball: roundhouse

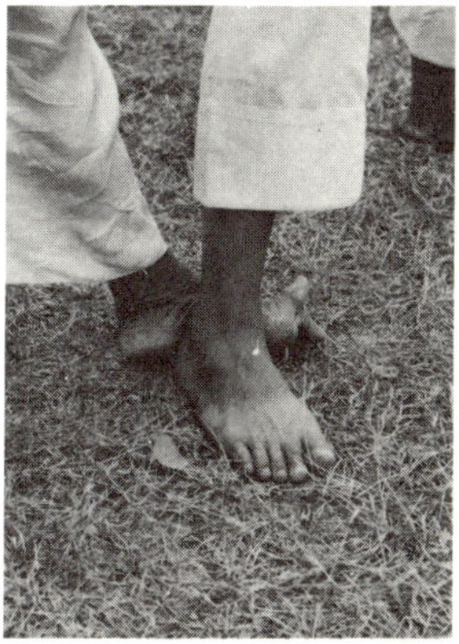

Sole

The Sole

When the whole undersurface of the foot, the sole, is used against an aggressor it is delivered with a forward thrust or pushing action. To form this weapon curl your toes upward and keep them in that position by maintaining tension in the upper part of your foot. When you wish to inflict direct punishment on the foe, thrust-kick your foot straight forward, with the toes pointing upward, against these recommended vital targets: mid-body areas (solar plexus, spine); lower-body areas (groin, buttocks).

When you wish to obstruct the foe's movement backward, hook the sole of your foot behind the enemy's foot, making contact with the heel of his foot in the Achilles region.

Instep

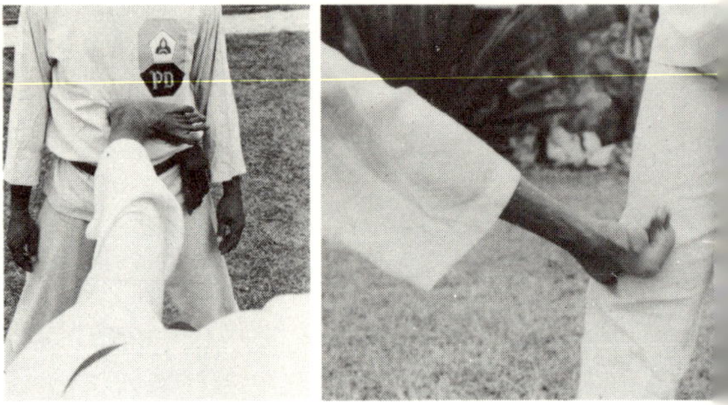

Heel: side thrust-kicks

The Instep

When you extend your foot to point your toes downward away from your body you expose the upper surface of the foot, the instep. This formation can be used as an effective weapon. Deliver it straight forward in a snap-kick that strikes the enemy's groin. Or use a rising kick that strikes upward against his testicles.

The Heel

Flex your foot to bring the toes upward and your instep closer to your shinbone. This action will jut your heel downward and expose it for striking; maintain this formation by keeping strength in the flexed ankle. Deliver the heel in either a side thrust-kick or reverse sickle-kick against the following recommended targets: mid-body areas (solar plexus, ribs, heart, liver, kidneys, spine); lower-body areas (groin); the kneecaps from the front, or from the outer or inner side of the knee.

The Outer Anklebone

Put strength in your little toe as you rotate your ankle to turn the sole inward; maintain this formation by keeping tension in the ankle. This action exposes the outer anklebone, which can be delivered in a crescent kick. This kind of delivery brings your leg laterally across the front of your body (a "backhand" delivery) in a short arc and is best applied against these recommended targets: mid-body areas (solar plexus, ribs, liver, kidneys, heart); lower-body areas (groin, inner and outer thigh muscles, inner and outer areas of the knee joints).

/: reverse sickle-kick

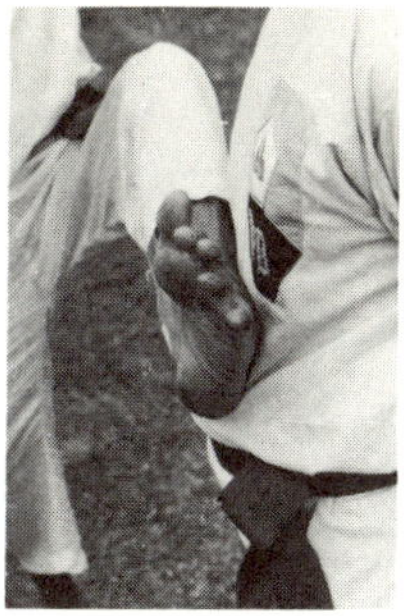

Outer anklebone

Inner anklebone

Shinbone

The Inner-edge and Anklebone

Extend your foot to point your toes downward and hold them in that position by means of tension in the foot. This is the same kind of preparation as you used with the instep. Deliver this formation in a roundhouse kick, turning your foot just enough to impact the inner surface of your foot from instep to shin. Use the anklebone as a contact surface against the following targets: mid-body areas (solar plexus, ribs, liver, kidneys); lower-body areas (groin, inner and outer thigh muscles, inner and outer areas of the knee joint).

The Shinbone

The basic use of the shinbone in the P.D. system is as part of a tactic to off-balance or obstruct an enemy. The foot, in conjunction with the shinbone, forms a hooklike appendage that can be used to trap the enemy's leg. Step flat onto the ground with your foot behind the enemy's; your foot must come into close contact with his. Wedge your shinbone up against the inner shin and ankle of the foe from a position inside his leg. As you do this, bend your knee and apply pressure against the portion of his leg that you have trapped. Forcefully press his leg downward by lunging forward over the leg you are using against him; twist your body a little bit to your free side as you lunge. Correctly done, this tactic will off-balance the foe and may crush him to the ground.

Calf

Knee: rising and roundhouse kicks

The Calf

The back portion of your leg at the calf can be a durable part of your anatomy if it is correctly used. When used against the enemy's lower-body regions, it is an effective weapon that will inflict punishment as well as cause the foe to lose his balance. Deliver the calf formation in a backward reap-kick and direct it against these targets: lower-body areas (groin; frontal, inner, and outer areas of the knee joints).

The Knee

The upper portion of the knee where it joins the thigh is one of the hardest surfaces found on the human body. Its use against vital weaknesses on the enemy's body, however, requires that you come into very close contact with the foe. Thus the knee must be used quickly and with full commitment to produce a decisive effect before the enemy can react.

Form the knee by extending your foot and pointing your toes downward, just as you did when making the instep formation; hold your foot in this position by means of tension throughout the foot. Deliver your knee either in a rising trajectory straight forward or in a roundhouse fashion against the following recommended targets: mid-body areas (solar plexus, ribs, liver, heart, kidneys, spine); lower-body areas (groin; frontal, inner, and outer thigh muscles).

5 TRAINING EXERCISES

Essential to silat technique is the P.D. exponent's mastery of a full range of self-defense responses that can be used in any kind of situation to put a dangerous aggressor at a disadvantage. The varieties of response have given P.D. its own very special characteristics, some of which are clearly reflected in the P.D. training exercises.

P.D. training exercises are of a composite nature. They consist of a series of individual actions embodied in what may be called silat sequences. Each silat sequence is to be performed in a fluid manner by the participating exponents—training partners—who are usually, though not necessarily, two in number. At the most basic level a training exercise contains only one silat sequence. At advanced levels training exercises consist of multiple silat sequences. No limit is set to the number of sequences that may be contained in a single exercise, but the usual maximum number is five or six in order to focus attention on the individual techniques that make up each sequence.

In the performance of a silat sequence the participants demonstrate their degree of control over P.D. fundamentals as they are used in self-defense techniques. A training exercise is, therefore, a splendid chance for each participant to improve stance and posture (sikap), displacement maneuvers, and the formation of anatomical weapons and the ways of using them. Each participant also learns just how an aggressor might launch an attack, and how it feels to be the intended victim of such an attack.

So that the training exercise may proceed in the manner and spirit for which it is designed, each participant is allowed to impose certain tactical "problems" on his partner; in turn, he must solve those problems that the partner imposes on him. The exponent must respond to an attack or defense in the manner that he judges best suits the situation, and is free to choose what specific techniques he will apply. There is no agreed on technique, or any one proper kind of technique, or an order of techniques in the course of a training exercise. Certain of the exponent's actions, however, will lead the silat sequence to its logical climax. These are styled "decisive actions"; that is, their goal is to cause the partner to submit and the exercise to terminate. If, however, the party against whom the decisive action is directed is able to evade or neutralize that action, the exercise will continue until such time as a conclusive decisive action can be made.

The P.D. training exercise is not a sterile situation based on prearranged movements having foregone conclusions. Rather, it is dynamically alive, changing with the situation and the techniques applied by the participants. The responses that can emerge in the course of a silat sequence are theoretically limitless. Moreover, the P.D. training exercise is designed to expose the participants to a wide variety of terrain, weather conditions, and other factors that might influence and determine the outcome of real combat. No conscious effort is made to provide convenient facilities or accommodating circumstances for the participants because such concessions are usually alien to the nature of real combat.

In spite of the great variety of techniques produced by the sequential action of any one training exercise, and no matter how high the degree of spirit of the participants or the severity under which they perform, the P.D. training exercise is not real combat. It is only an approximation of the real thing. The presence of extreme danger to life and limb must unfailingly be recognized and dealt with in silat training. This is especially true when weapons are used. Every exponent must constantly use good judgment in carrying out his actions against his training partner; he is responsible for his safety. But injuries can, and do, occur when the degree of control of technique weakens or is ignored altogether. Thus the method by which the P.D. training exercise is to be carried out becomes of great importance to all P.D. exponents, who are expected to abide by the spirit and letter of silat ethics.

THE METHOD OF THE P.D. TRAINING EXERCISE

In its most basic form the P.D. training exercise is performed by two training partners. It is this type of training exercise that is presented in this book. For the purpose of making a clear explanation these two exponents are simply designated as A and B. At the start of an exercise the exponents assume standard P.D. combative attitudes (sikap) and mutually adjust the distance that lies between them. Either party may initiate the action, thus becoming the initial aggressor. Thereafter, the role of the attacker may change hands if the other party is able to gain the attack initiative. He may gain this initiative, lose it, then recapture it several times before a conclusive decisive action terminates the exercise. It is not essential that one particular party emerge the "victor" at the end of the exercise. Either exponent may become "victorious" by rendering a conclusive decisive action which makes it clear to both participants that one of them is unable to continue because of his decidedly inferior position. The decision as to who will be the first aggressor at the start of the exercise rests with the exponent who can best approximate the spirit of an actual aggressor and who is able to find an opening or weakness in his intended victim's mental or physical attitude.

Once action begins each exponent performs what preliminary movements are necessary—displacements for making or evading an attack—as he seeks decisive action. Decisive action can be achieved by punching, striking, butting, kicking, kneeing, throwing, or locking the other party. Often a decisive action consists of two separate techniques executed simultaneously or in swift succession. For example, the exponent may kick and punch or strike at the same instant in an attempt to take decisive action against his partner. At this time the intended victim is given the opportunity to take instant and appropriate countermeasures, to respond to the attack with a suitable technique of his own and, eventually, should he be able to steal the attack initiative away from his partner, to take decisive action himself. In this manner the training exercise continues through a number of silat sequences until one of the exponents fails to make a response that either neutralizes or allows him to evade his partner's attack.

All the training exercises that follow in the remaining pages of this chapter are model exercises that are typical of the P.D. system. These exercises have, for the trainee's convenience, been divided into exercises of one, two, three, four, and five sequences. Occasionally, alternate sequences are provided to show what might happen if one of the partners were to choose a different response to a defense problem. Through practice of these exercises the trainee will gain familiarity with the fundamentals of

P.D. silat. And with sufficient practice he will develop a creditable silat technique that will stand him in good stead should he have to apply his technique in the defense of his person.

The exercises may be practiced in any order, but for obvious reasons those with fewer sequences should be attempted first. Repetition—performing a single chosen exercise over and over a number of times—is preferable to casual practice. When any one exercise can be performed fluently in the precise manner described a new exercise may then be attempted. Trainees are advised not to elaborate or change the established form of the exercises at least until their skill is such that variations become necessary. In time the exponent may wish to design his own training exercises, basing them on the fundamentals he has acquired through the practice of the standard exercises offered here.

The photographs that accompany the training exercises will help the trainee understand the motions described in the text. They will also show how different stances, postures, and techniques are modified to suit particular combat situations. Owing to the high speed at which training exercises are performed it has not always been possible to include photographs that show each stage of the action or each of the many different techniques that occur almost simultaneously. The photographs are primarily a guide, and in all cases the trainee should take the text as an authority and read it carefully to interpolate between the techniques pictured. The boldface numbers preceded by black diamonds indicate the photographs that correspond to the text.

TRAINING EXERCISES

SINGLE-SEQUENCE TRAINING EXERCISES

1

2

TRAINING EXERCISE 1

Preparation

◆1. A (left) stands in *sikap putri* and threatens B, who assumes *sikap pendeta.*

Silat Sequence

◆2, 3. A leaps directly at B, landing on his right leg. He delivers a side thrust-kick, aiming his left heel at B's solar plexus.

◆4, 5. B evades the kick by stepping and lunging sideways over his right leg; at the same time, B brings both hands held in claw-hand formation against the outside of A's kicking leg near the ankle, deflecting it to B's left.

◆6. Thereupon, B assumes *sikap garuda* while A takes advantage of the force of deflection to turn his body completely around to his right by using his platform right leg as an axle.

◆7, 8. A takes decisive action. He cross-steps his raised left leg in front of him, shifts his weight onto that leg, and steps with his right foot to a position between B's outstretched legs; at the same time A delivers his right forearm-elbow in a backhand chop to B's throat to end the exercise.

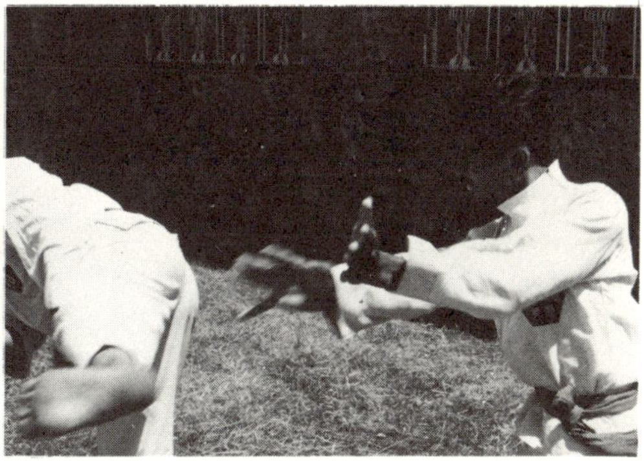

4

5

6

7

8

1

2

3

4

5

6

TRAINING EXERCISE 2

Preparation

◆**1.** A (farthest from camera) assumes *sikap burung kuntul,* to which threat B responds by taking *sikap pendeta.*

Silat Sequence

◆**2, 3.** A closes with B by turning to his right and stepping with his raised right leg to the ground. He delivers a side thrust-kick with his left heel aimed at B's advanced left knee joint.

◆**4.** B escapes A's kick by quickly turning his body around to his left, thus bringing his target left leg around in an arc in the same direction; he assumes *sikap putri.*

◆**5.** A retracts his kicking leg, but before he can continue his attack, B steals the initiative and takes decisive action. B quickly cross-steps his left leg in front of him and to his right in order to close with A.

◆**6.** Using his left leg as a platform, B delivers a side thrust-kick that impacts the heel of his right foot against the inner area of A's platform right leg at the knee joint; this ends the exercise.

1

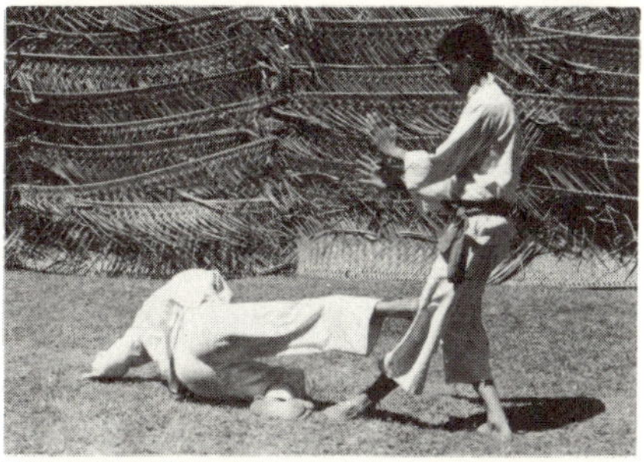

2

3

4

5

TRAINING EXERCISE 3

Preparation

◆1. A (left) threatens B from *sikap putri.* B meets the threat in *sikap putri.*

Silat Sequence

◆2. A dives at B, feet first, and delivers a side thrust-kick with his right heel aimed at the front portion of B's advanced left knee.

◆3, 4. An instant before A can focus his kick B leaps sideways to his left and assumes *sikap naga;* he stands on his left leg, his right leg is bent and raised.

◆5. Before A can recover, B hops on his left leg to his right side into a position nearer A, who is still on the ground. B then takes decisive action to end the exercise by delivering a side thrust-kick with his right heel to the right side of A's head.

1 2 3 4 5

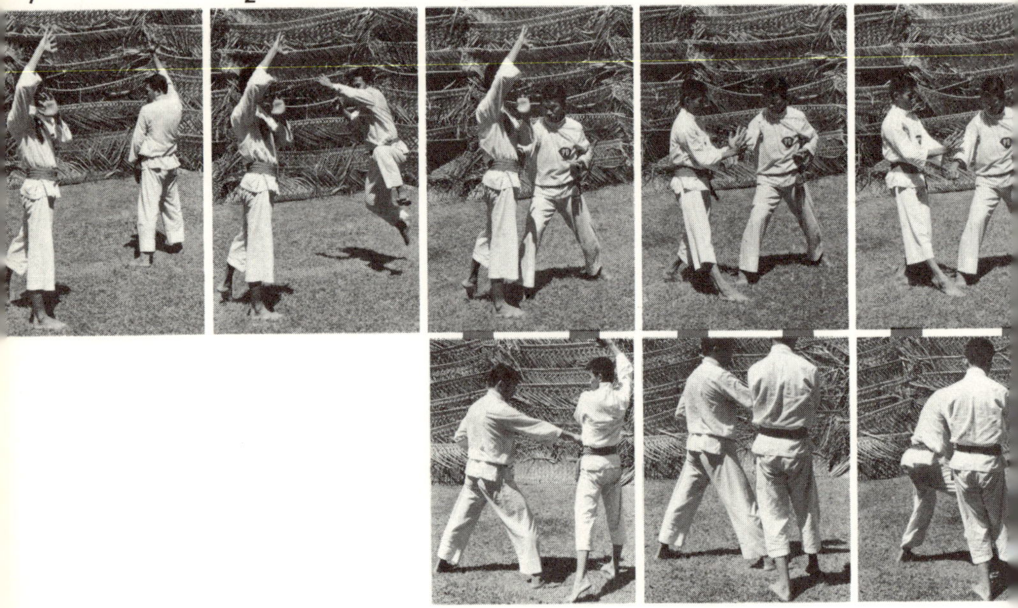

TRAINING EXERCISE 4

Preparation

◆1. A (right) threatens B from *sikap naga* as B stands in *sikap garuda.*

Silat Sequence

◆2, 3. A jumps directly at B and delivers a thrust-punch with his clenched right fist to assault B's left rib cage.

◆4, 5. B evades the punch by quickly rocking his weight back over his rear left leg, thus removing his mid-body area from the line of the punch; at the same time B brings the knife-edges of both hands vertically downward to deflect A's punching arm at the wrist.

7

8

9

10

11

◆6, 7. A uses the downward force generated by B's deflection to slide his advanced right foot behind B's advanced right foot, there to use his shinbone in an attempt to trap B's foot and restrict his movement; at the same time A bends forward and attempts to attack B's right leg and, by so doing, send B to the ground. With his left hand A grasps and pulls B's right leg near the ankle as he uses his right forearm-elbow to push against B's leg just above the knee.

◆8, 9. B leaps sideways to his right to escape and assumes *sikap putri.*

◆10, 11. Before A can recover B takes decisive action. He leaps directly at A to deliver the heel of his right foot against the right side of A's neck; at the same time B delivers his clenched fist in a right thrust-punch that is aimed just a bit higher than A's head, in case A should attempt to rise and B's kick miss its intended mark. This ends the exercise.

7′ 8′ 9′

Alternate Silat Sequence

Should A manage to pick up B's right leg at the point of the sequence shown in ◆7, B can exercise the following option.

◆7′, 8′. A scoops up B's right leg, cradling it in the crook of his right arm.

◆9′. But B swings his captured right leg upward, faster than A is lifting it, and attempts to take it off of A's arm.

◆10′. A foils B's attempt by suddenly twisting, feet in place, to his right; in so doing he swings both arms to his right and flings B's captured leg in that direction. A then assumes *sikap pendeta.*

◆11′, 12′. B takes advantage of the force of deflection by using his left leg as an axle and turning completely around to his left; as B comes around to face A, B stamps his raised right leg to the ground and, using that leg as a platform, raises his left leg to assume *sikap burung kuntul.*

◆13′. B takes decisive action. He steps forward with his left leg to position that foot between A's feet; at the same time, B uses his left beak-hand to peck into A's left eye, thus ending the exercise.

11'

12'

13'

TWO-SEQUENCE TRAINING EXERCISES

1

2

3

6

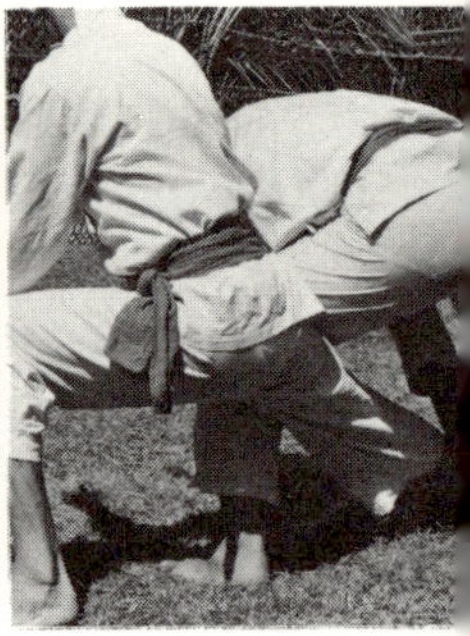
7

TRAINING EXERCISE 5

Preparation

◆1. A (right) stands in *sikap setria* and threatens B, who assumes *sikap pendeta.*

Silat Sequence 1

◆**2, 3.** A closes with B and from a left stance delivers his clenched left fist in backhand fashion, aiming it at the left side of B's head.

◆**4.** B evades this blow; using his right leg as an axle he pivots around backward to his left and swings his left leg around behind him in an arc. At the same time, B uses the claw-hand formations of both hands to deflect A's oncoming punch to his left.

5

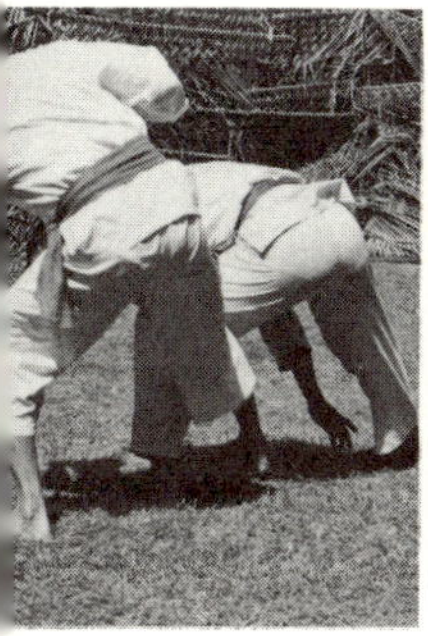

9

10

11

◆**5.** Immediately B takes *sikap harimau*; A takes *sikap setria.*
◆**6, 7.** A continues his attack by stepping in front of B's right leg with his left leg; then, reaching down, he attempts to pick up B's right leg by grabbing it at the ankle.
◆**8, 9.** B quickly withdraws his target right leg; he swings it around in an arc to his rear and raises and bends his left leg to assume *sikap setria.* A remains in a bent-over posture, but keeps his eye on B.
◆**10, 11.** Instantly B takes decisive action. He stamps his left leg down, using his left heel against A's spine; he then lowers that leg to the ground and places his left foot near A as he uses his arms to deliver both forearm-elbows straight down in chopping fashion to the base of A's skull.

12

13

14

15

16

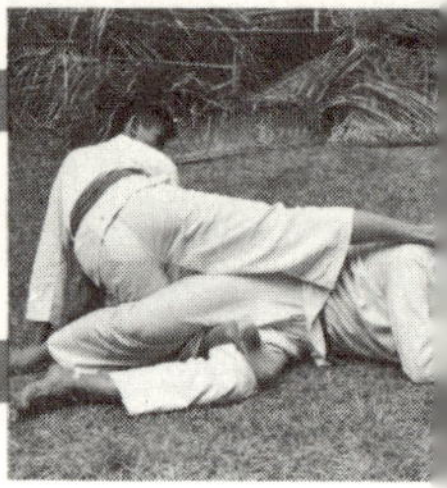

Silaṭ Sequence 2

◆12, 13, 14. A evades the focus of the blow by diving face forward to the ground to his right, where he supports himself on both hands. Instantly he thrusts both legs backward; he positions his left leg behind B's advanced left leg near the ankle, and his right leg higher up on B's left leg just above the knee.

◆15. With a twist of his body to his right, A uses his legs in a shearing action against B's trapped left leg and topples B sideward and backward to the ground.

◆16. B takes decisive action. Upon falling he delivers a side thrust-kick with his right heel to the right side of A's head to end the exercise.

2

3

4

5

6

7

TRAINING EXERCISE 6

Preparation

◆**1.** A (left) stands in *sikap putri* and menaces B, who is in *sikap putri.*

Silat Sequence 1

◆**2, 3.** A leaps forward at B; after landing on his left leg he delivers a right roundhouse kick, aiming his inner anklebone at B's ribs on the left side.

◆**4, 5.** B deflects A's kick to his right by using the forearm-elbows of both his arms against A's kicking leg near the ankle. B immediately assumes *sikap setria;* A, taking advantage of the force of the deflection to bring his kicking leg forward to the ground, takes decisive action.

◆**6, 7.** A turns around to his right using his right leg as an axle and delivers a straight thrust-kick with his left heel aimed at B's left ribs.

8

9

10

11

12

Silat Sequence 2

◆8. Before A's kick can make contact, B deflects the kicking leg to his left by bringing the forearm-elbows of both his arms against A's leg from the outside near the ankle; B turns to his left to reinforce that action and assumes *sikap putri.* A takes advantage of the force of deflection to turn his body a bit to the right; he retracts his kicking leg but keeps it in a raised position, bent at the knee.

◆9. Before A can continue his attack, B dives under A's raised left leg by shifting his weight forward onto his advanced left leg and stepping with his right leg across the front of A's platform right leg. B then uses his right shoulder in an attempt to unbalance A by pushing upward against the underside of A's buttocks.

◆10. A takes advantage of the attempt to unbalance him by riding the force of the push and leaping forward, away from B.

◆11. B remains in a low crouching posture as A assumes *sikap naga.*

◆12. B takes decisive action. He swings his retreated left leg in an arc behind him to position his left foot in front of A's left foot; he then shifts his weight onto his left leg, and, using that leg as a platform, delivers a crescent kick so that his right outer anklebone strikes against A's solar plexus. This ends the exercise.

2

3

5

6

7

TRAINING EXERCISE 7

Preparation

◆1. A (left) threatens B from *sikap setria.* B stands motionless in *sikap harimau.*

Silat Sequence 1

◆**2, 3.** A steps forward onto his left leg and delivers a thrust-kick with the sole of his right foot aimed at the left side of B's head.

◆**4.** B evades the kick by suddenly standing up straight just before the kick can be focused. Keeping his feet in place, B turns his body to his left and, while doing so, deflects A's kicking leg to the left with the forearm-elbow of his left arm.

◆**5, 6.** Following through with the deflecting action, B swings his left leg back around in a short arc behind him and, turning a bit more to his left, assumes *sikap naga;* at the same time, A retracts his kicking leg but keeps it raised in the air.

◆**7.** A takes decisive action. He stamps his raised right leg to the ground and steps forward onto his left leg to close with B, so that his left foot is behind B's advanced right foot. A delivers his clenched left fist in backhand fashion to B's mouth.

8

9

10

11

12

Silat Sequence 2

◆**8, 9.** B evades A's backhand blow by turning to his right. He steps with his right leg to his right rear side and, as he turns, deflects A's striking arm with the outer surface of his upper right arm (above the elbow).

◆**10.** A holds his ground but assumes *sikap setria* as B takes *sikap putri.*

◆**11, 12.** A takes decisive action. He steps forward with his retreated right leg and positions that foot in front of and between B's feet; he then delivers his clenched right fist in a hammer-blow to the left side of B's head. This ends the exercise.

8′

9′

10′

11′

12′

Alternate Silat Sequence 2

◆8′, 9′, 10′. B may steal the attack initiative after he deflects A's backhand blow and before A can take decisive action. These photos show B's deflection of A's backhand blow from a different camera angle.

◆11′, 12′. Before A can step forward to take decisive action, however, B leaps forward directly at A and delivers a side thrust-kick using his left heel against A's solar plexus to end the exercise.

THREE-SEQUENCE TRAINING EXERCISES

1

2

3

4

TRAINING EXERCISE 8

Preparation

◆1. A (left) assumes *sikap putri* and confronts B, who stands in *sikap putri*.

Silat Sequence 1

◆**2.** A launches his attack by stepping forward onto his left leg and delivering a side thrust-kick with the heel of his right foot aimed at B's solar plexus.

◆**3.** B deflects A's kicking leg to his right by turning his body to the right and using the forearm-elbow of his left arm to make contact on the outside of A's leg near the ankle.

◆**4, 5.** B remains in place but A steps down with his kicking leg to position his right foot between B's feet from in front of B. At the same time, A takes decisive action. He delivers his clenched right fist in backhand fashion against B's groin.

6

7

8

Silat Sequence 2

◆6. B evades A's backhand blow by deflecting it downward with his right palm-hand near the wrist; with his left palm hand he jabs against the right side of A's head. At the same time he leaps, left leg first, to his left rear corner.

◆7. B lands on his left leg and assumes *sikap burung kuntul;* A remains in place but watches B from the corner of his eye.

◆8. B takes the initiative. He jumps forward to a position directly behind A and lands on both feet, his right leg forward; B pushes with both palms against A's buttocks.

9

10

11

12

13

◆**9, 10, 11.** A uses the force of B's push to turn quickly in place to his right; he steps around the right side of B and assumes *sikap naga.*

◆**12, 13.** B takes immediate decisive action. He shifts his weight forward onto his advanced right leg and turns around to his left to deliver the heel of his left foot into A's groin with a reverse sickle-kick; at the same time he aims his left forearm-elbow in backhand fashion against the right side of A's neck.

14

15

16

17

Silat Sequence 3

◆**14.** A evades the kick and the blow by driving forward over his advanced right leg and using his right shoulder to shove B off-balance.

◆**15.** B evades that shove by withdrawing his left leg and pivoting around to his right; he stamps his left foot down onto the ground, shifts his weight onto that leg, and assumes *sikap burung kuntul.*

◆**16, 17.** Before A can react B takes decisive action. He delivers a crescent kick, using the outer anklebone of his right foot against A's spine (lumbar); at the same time, he delivers the knife-edge of his right hand in backhand fashion to the base of A's skull. This ends the exercise.

1

2

3

4

5

6

TRAINING EXERCISE 9

Preparation

◆**1.** A (nearer camera) stands in *sikap burung kuntul* and threatens B, who assumes *sikap naga.*

Silat Sequence 1

◆**2.** A leaps forward at B; landing on his right leg, A turns to his right and delivers a roundhouse kick with his left inner ankle-bone aimed at B's groin.

◆**3, 4.** B evades the kick by pivoting around to his left on his right leg and swinging his retreated left leg in an arc behind him; at the same time, B covers his groin with his left hand and brushes the palm of his right hand against A's kicking leg near the ankle to deflect the kick downward. B assumes *sikap setria;* A remains standing on his right leg, his kicking left leg withdrawn.

◆**5, 6.** A takes immediate decisive action. He leaps toward B, springs off his left foot, and lands behind B, where he delivers his right forearm-elbow in driving fashion to the right side of B's head.

5′

6′

7′

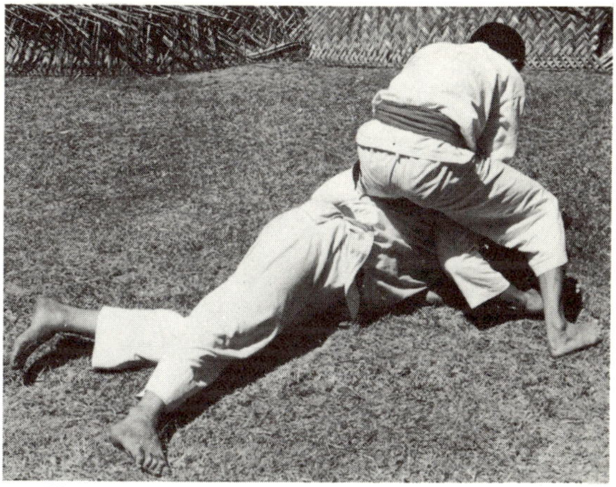

8′

Alternate Silat Sequence 1

◆**5′, 6′, 7′, 8′.** A may elect to take more drastic decisive action. At the time of his leap at B he may go around behind B in order to seize B's head in both hands and execute the eye tear and neck twist, thereby hurling B around and down to the ground to end the exercise.

7

8

9

10

11

Silat Sequence 2

◆7, 8, 9. At the time that A is delivering his right forearm-elbow to the right side of B's head (◆6), B suddenly pivots around to his right side by swinging his right leg around in an arc to his right rear corner; at the same time, he brushes A's striking arm off its intended course by using the outer surface of his own upraised right arm on the underside of A's arm (above the elbow). B assumes *sikap naga* after this action.

◆10, 11. B then takes immediate decisive action. He shifts his weight forward onto his left leg and delivers a roundhouse kick with the instep of his right foot aimed at A's solar plexus.

12

13

15

16

Silat Sequence 3

◆**12, 13, 14.** A evades the roundhouse kick by turning his body to his right and leaping backward to assume *sikap putri;* B retracts his kicking leg.

◆**15, 16.** B thereupon takes further decisive action to end the exercise. As he steps forward onto his right leg he delivers his right forearm-elbow in backhand fashion against the left side of A's neck.

1

2

3

4

5

6

TRAINING EXERCISE 10

Preparation

◆**1.** A (right) is moving forward out of *sikap burung kuntul* against B, who stands in *sikap pendeta.*

Silat Sequence 1

◆**2.** A stamps his raised right leg to the ground and delivers a roundhouse kick aiming his left inner anklebone at B's groin.

◆**3.** Before A can focus the kick, B evades it by shifting his weight onto his right leg and turning to his left; he swings his advanced left leg around in an arc to his left side; at the same time he deflects A's kicking leg to his left by using the palms of both hands against the outer surface of A's kicking leg near the ankle.

◆**4, 5.** Thereupon B assumes *sikap garuda.* A takes advantage of the force of deflection to turn all the way around to his right while holding his retracted kicking leg bent at the knee in the air. As he comes to face B, A stamps his raised left leg to the ground and raises his right leg to assume *sikap burning kuntul.*

◆**6.** A takes decisive action. He steps down with his raised right leg and positions his right foot near the inside of A's left foot; at the same time he delivers a double thrust-punch with both hands formed as arrowhead fists against the right side of B's neck.

7

8

9

10

Silat Sequence 2

◆7. B evades the double thrust-punch by, feet in place, quickly twisting his upper body to his right; at the same time, he deflects A's punching arms to his right by using the knife-edges of both hands near A's wrists.

◆8. With this deflection B assumes *sikap putri.* A uses the force of deflection to his own advantage by assuming *sikap pendeta.*

◆9, 10. B takes decisive action. He suddenly shifts his weight onto his advanced right leg and delivers a crescent kick aiming his left outer anklebone against A's solar plexus; he simultaneously delivers the fingers of his open left hand in whip fashion into A's face.

11

12

13

14

15

Silat Sequence 3

◆11. A escapes B's kick and hand blow by shifting his weight onto his rear left leg and lowering his body a bit; he steps forward with his right leg to a position under B's kicking left leg and, at the same time, drives his right forearm-elbow against the shinbone of B's kicking leg to deflect it downward. While so doing, A covers his mid-body area with his right arm and protects himself from B's whip strike by covering his face with the palm of his left hand.

◆12, 13. A now dives under B's kicking leg and uses his right shoulder to butt upward and forward against the back of B's left thigh, sending B sprawling face down to the ground.

◆14. B falls to the ground, where A seeks to immobilize him by locking B's right leg with his own right leg and pressing against B's buttocks with both hands.

◆15. But A, who is supporting himself on both hands, takes decisive action to end the exercise by delivering a reverse sickle-kick with his left heel against A's face.

1

2

3

4

TRAINING EXERCISE 11

Preparation

◆1. A (right) threatens B from *sikap putri.* B stands in *sikap pendeta.*

Silat Sequence 1

◆2, 3. A suddenly jumps forward onto his right leg and delivers a side thrust-kick with his left heel aimed at B's solar plexus.

◆4. B evades the kick an instant before it makes contact. He sidesteps wide to his right side with his right leg, then lunges over that leg and deflects A's kicking leg to the left with the palms of both hands.

5

6

7

8

9

10

11

◆5. B assumes *sikap putri* as A blends with the force of B's deflection to turn to his right and stand momentarily on his right leg; he raises and bends his left leg.

◆6, 7. Immediately A jumps up and around in place to his left to land on his left leg and take decisive action. From his platform left leg A jumps directly at B to deliver a right forearm-elbow strike in backhand fashion aimed at B's face.

Silat Sequence 2

◆8, 9, 10. B evades A's backhand strike by leaping backward, right foot leading, and turning to his right, where he assumes *sikap pendeta.*

◆11. Before A can recover, B takes decisive action. He leaps directly at A onto his advanced left leg, positioning his left foot behind and between A's two feet; at the same instant, B delivers a double thrust-punch, his semiclenched fists formed as arrow-head fists, to the right side of A's neck.

12

13

14

15

16

17

Silat Sequence 3

◆**12, 13, 14.** A evades B's double thrust-punch by quickly turning around to his right. He pivots on his left leg and brings his right leg back and around in a short arc to his right rear corner; simultaneously he uses the forearm-elbows of both arms to deflect B's punching arms to his right.

◆**15.** B avails himself of the force of the deflection to lower his body and launch an attack against A. B attempts to unbalance A by diving under him and pushing with his right shoulder in the hope of knocking him to the ground.

◆**16.** A now takes decisive action to end the exercise. A evades B's push by withdrawing his right leg and stepping to his rear; while doing so he grasps B's head in both hands.

◆**17.** A executes the eye tear and neck twist to swing B around to the right and hurl him around and face down to the ground.

The above photos, taken from a different angle, show the steps in A's execution of the eye tear and neck twist that brings B to the ground to end the exercise.

FOUR-SEQUENCE TRAINING EXERCISES

1

2

3

TRAINING EXERCISE 12

Preparation

◆1. A (left) stands in *sikap putri* and threatens B, who assumes *sikap putri.*

Silat Sequence 1

◆2. A closes with B by stepping forward onto his left leg; he delivers a side thrust-kick with his right heel aimed at B's solar plexus.

◆3. But this kick is only a ruse that A intentionally focuses short of its implied target. Quickly A steps to the ground with his kicking right leg and positions his right foot in front of and between B's feet; at that instant A attempts to drive his right shoulder into B in order to knock B backward.

4

5

6

◆**4, 5.** B evades the shove by leaping away to his left side; he lands on his left leg and raises his right leg, bending it at the knee, as A assumes *sikap garuda.*

◆**6.** B steals the attack initiative by immediately stepping forward onto his right leg, which he places directly behind A; he attempts to shove A forward by using both hands placed against A's buttocks or lower back.

◆**7, 8.** A responds to the shove by making use of its force to pivot on his right leg around to his right; as he comes around behind B, A assumes *sikap naga.*

◆**9, 10.** B takes decisive action by quickly shifting his weight onto his advanced right leg and delivering a reverse sickle-kick with the heel of his left foot aimed at A's groin; simultaneously he delivers his left forearm-elbow in backhand fashion against the right side of A's head.

8 9 10

11 12 13

Silat Sequence 2

◆11. A counters B's reverse sickle-kick by stepping in close to B and butting his right hip up against the underside of B's left buttock; this action knocks B off-balance and negates the force of his kick.

◆12. B quickly recovers his balance by slipping away out of contact with A; he withdraws his kicking left leg and turns around to his right. As his left leg comes free of contact with A he stamps it to the ground and raises his right leg, which he bends at the knee.

◆13. B takes decisive action. He jumps around to his right to face A and, while standing on his platform left leg, delivers the knife-edge of his right hand in backhand fashion to the base of A's skull.

14

15

16

17

Silat Sequence 3

◆14. A defends against B's backhand blow by turning around to his right; he swings his right leg backward in an arc and simultaneously uses the palms of both hands to deflect B's blow to the right.

◆15. A assumes *sikap garuda* while B avails himself of the force of A's deflection to turn completely around to his left on his platform left leg.

◆16. B thereupon opens the interval between himself and A; he leaps to his right side and onto his right leg, from where he moves further back by turning around to his left to face A in *sikap putri.*

◆17. A takes decisive action. He leaps at B, landing on his right leg, and delivers a crescent kick with the outer anklebone of his left foot aimed at B's solar plexus.

18

19

Silat Sequence 4

◆**18.** B evades the kick and takes decisive action to end the exercise. Before A can focus his crescent kick B lunges onto his right leg and positions his right foot behind A; B lowers his body and deflects A's kicking leg to his left with the palms of both hands.

◆**19.** Immediately B delivers his left arrowhead fist under A's upraised, but now retracted, kicking leg and into A's groin; he presses his right palm up against the side of A's left buttock to impede the lowering of that leg. This ends the exercise.

1

2

3

7

8

9

TRAINING EXERCISE 13

Preparation

◆**1.** A (left) threatens to attack from *sikap putri* as B assumes *sikap putri.*

Silat Sequence 1

◆**2, 3.** A steps forward onto his left leg and launches a thrust-kick straight forward with the heel of his right foot aimed at B's solar plexus; at the same time, he delivers his clenched right fist in a backhand strike aimed at B's face.

◆**4.** B avoids A's attack by deflecting the kick outward to his left; while he brings the forearm-elbows of both arms against the inside of A's kicking leg below the knee he pivots on his feet and twists his upper body to his left.

◆**5.** B assumes *sikap harimau* as A takes advantage of the force of deflection to turn a bit to his right, where he retracts his kicking right leg and stamps it to the ground.

5

6

11

12

◆6. Using that leg as a platform A quickly delivers a crescent kick using the outer anklebone of his left foot against B's solar plexus.

◆7. B neutralizes this kick and forestalls any decisive action on A's part by bringing both arms under A's kicking leg near the ankle and catching it in the cradle formed by his arms.

◆8. Before B can take the initiative A disengages his kicking left leg from B's arms; to do this he lifts his left leg high and quickly retracts it, bending it at the knee.

◆9, 10. A begins to take decisive action. As A is stamping his raised left leg to the ground, B senses the threat and opens the interval between them by turning backward to his right and swinging his right leg around in a wide arc to assume *sikap harimau.*

◆11, 12. A leaps from his now lowered left leg directly at B; leading with his right leg he delivers his clenched right fist straight forward in a thrust-punch aimed at the left side of B's neck.

13

14

15

19

20

21

Silat Sequence 2

◆13. B evades A's thrust-punch by suddenly turning around to his left. He swings his outstretched left leg around in a very short arc to his left and at the same time uses the palm of his right hand against the wrist of A's punching right arm to deflect that arm downward and out to the left. B keeps his mid-body areas covered with his left hand.

◆14. B then assumes *sikap putri.*

◆15, 16. Before A can recover B takes decisive action. He quickly shifts his weight onto his advanced left leg and delivers a crescent kick using his right outer anklebone against A's solar plexus; simultaneously B delivers the knife-edge of his right hand at A's face.

Silat Sequence 3

◆17. A avoids the kick by closing the interval between himself and B; he brings his retreated left leg forward across B's front and drives his left shoulder against B both to neutralize B's striking arm and in an attempt to topple B to the ground.

◆18. But B avoids the contact; he quickly disengages his kicking right leg and steps it wide to his right rear corner, where he assumes *sikap naga.*

17

18

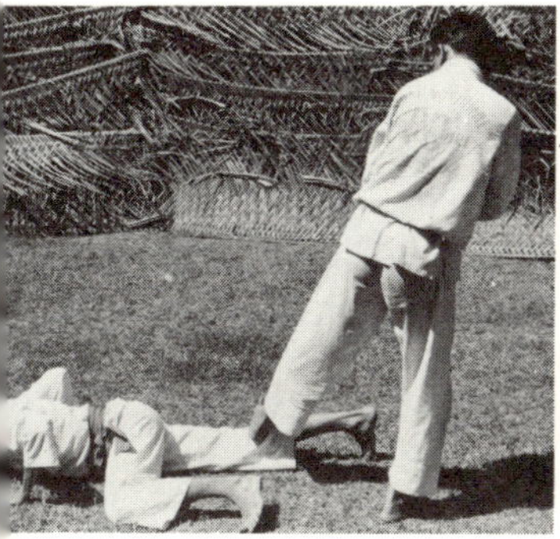

23

24

◆**19.** Now B takes decisive action before A can react. B leaps, left leg forward, to a position directly behind A and delivers his left forearm-elbow in backhand fashion to the base of A's skull.

Silat Sequence 4

◆**20.** A escapes from B's striking attack; before B can make contact, A pivots on his left leg, turning to his left and stepping around behind B with his right leg.

◆**21.** A quickly stamps his right leg to the ground and delivers a side thrust-kick with his left heel against the rear surface of B's right knee joint.

◆**22.** This kick sends B sprawling face down to the ground.

◆**23, 24.** A then takes decisive action. He leaps to his left side onto his left leg and, using that as a platform, delivers a side thrust-kick with his right heel against the left side of B's head to end the exercise.

FIVE-SEQUENCE TRAINING EXERCISES

1 *2*

3 *4* *5*

TRAINING EXERCISE 14

Preparation

◆1. A (left) and B face each other in mutual *sikap harimau.*

Silat Sequence 1

◆2. A suddenly steps forward onto his left leg. He delivers a straight thrust-punch with his clenched right fist aimed at B's face.

◆3. B evades the punch by turning his body slightly to his left and deflects A's punching arm from the inside with his left claw-hand.

◆4, 5. A immediately takes decisive action. Using the force of deflection he turns his body around to his right and swings his right leg in a backward arc in order to deliver his right forearm-elbow in backhand fashion into B's throat.

7 8 9

11 12

Silat Sequence 2

◆6. Keeping his feet in place, B evades A's blow by rocking his upper body back away from the attack while shoving the palm of his left hand against the back surface of A's right shoulder.

◆7. B then quickly steps back with his right leg and assumes *sikap garuda.*

◆8, 9. A continues the attack. He steps backward with his right leg so that it is just in front of and between B's outstretched legs and dives down in an attempt to pick up B's left leg.

◆10, 11. B avoids A's attack by withdrawing and swinging his target left leg in an arc to his rear; he assumes *sikap garuda.* A remains in a bent-over posture.

◆12. B then takes decisive action. He steps forward, positioning his right leg in front of A, and delivers the knife-edge of his right hand to the base of A's skull.

13

14

15

Silat Sequence 3

◆**13.** A evades that blow by suddenly rising and stepping around behind B.

◆**14, 15.** He shoves B's right shoulder with the palms of both hands as he swings his right leg around in a backward arc and assumes *sikap garuda.* B avails himself of the force of A's push to turn completely around to his left. B then takes decisive action. As he faces A, B steps forward onto his right leg and uses it as a platform as he delivers a roundhouse kick to impact the inner-anklebone area of his left foot into A's solar plexus.

6

17

18

19

20

Silat Sequence 4

◆**16, 17.** A turns away from the kick by quickly swinging his advanced left leg around in an arc behind him; at the same time, he deflects the kick to his left by sinking into a deep crouching posture and using the forearm-elbows of both arms against B's left leg.

◆**18.** B retracts his kicking left leg and assumes *sikap burung kuntul.*

◆**19, 20.** B takes decisive action. He turns to his left, stamps his raised left leg to the ground, and then steps forward with his right leg in order to close with A; he delivers the knife-edge of his right hand straight down from overhead to the base of A's skull.

21

22

23

24

25

Silat Sequence 5

◆21. A evades the blow by quickly pivoting on his right leg and stepping around and behind B with his left leg.

◆22. A takes decisive action by reaching down and attacking B's outstretched left leg.

◆23. A picks up that leg with both hands and raises it high in the air to send B sprawling headfirst to the ground.

◆24, 25. A retains his hold on B's captured leg and steps forward to position his right leg under B's left leg. By keeping an upward pressure on B's captured leg A causes B to submit; this ends the exercise.

1

3

2

4

5

TRAINING EXERCISE 15

Preparation

◆1. A (left) stands in *sikap setria* and is menacing B, who meets the threat in a natural posture.

Silat Sequence 1

◆2. As A prepares to leap forward at B, B suddenly assumes *sikap harimau.*

◆3, 4, 5. A's forward leap brings him onto his left leg, which he uses as a platform while he delivers a thrust-kick straight forward, aiming the sole of his right foot at B's solar plexus.

6

7

8

9

10

◆6, 7. A follows the kick by using his clenched right fist in a thrust-punch aimed at B's face. B avoids A's attack by suddenly pivoting, feet in place, to twist his body around to his left, where he assumes *sikap naga;* he covers his mid-body areas with his right hand and arm while he deflects A's kick upward and outward by raising his left arm overhead in a circular flinging action from inside A's kicking leg.

◆8. B maintains *sikap naga* but steps with his left leg to his left side; A takes advantage of the force of B's deflection by retracting his kicking right leg and then quickly stepping with it to the ground.

◆9, 10. A takes decisive action. From his right leg he leaps at B and delivers a backhand blow with his clenched left fist aimed at the right side of B's head.

Silat Sequence 2

◆11, 12. B escapes A's backhand strike by rocking his upper body back and away from the oncoming blow; at the same time, he steps with his right foot to position it directly behind A's advanced left foot. Turning to his right, B raises his right arm, bent at the elbow, to deflect A's striking arm from inside and below.

12

13

14

15

16

◆**13.** B now swings his right leg around in a big arc to his rear as he flings his right arm in that direction in order to misdirect A's striking arm; B's right arm covers his mid-body line in front of him as he raises his left arm high overhead to temporarily assume *sikap naga*. A remains immobile.

◆**14.** As soon as B changes to *sikap garuda*, A takes decisive action. A steps forward onto his right leg to position his right foot in front of B's left foot; he then delivers a downward hammer-blow with his clenched right fist to the left side of B's head.

Silat Sequence 3

◆**15.** B evades A's hammer-blow by stepping backward with his left leg; at the same time, he brings the claw-hand formations of both hands against the inside of A's striking arm near the wrist and flings that arm to his left. B then opens the interval between himself and A by pivoting on his left leg and bringing his right leg around in an arc to his right rear. A takes advantage of the force of B's deflection to turn to his right; he steps in an arc to his rear with his advanced right leg and allows his deflected arm to rise to a position overhead as he assumes *sikap setria*.

◆**16.** B takes decisive action. He steps forward onto his right leg and from that platform delivers a side thrust-kick to impact his left heel against A's solar plexus.

17

18

19

23

24

25

Silat Sequence 4

◆**17.** A avoids B's kick by twisting his upper body, feet in place, to the left and deflects the kick in that direction with the palm of his right hand; he assumes *sikap garuda.* B uses the force of deflection to spin completely around to his right, using his platform right leg as an axle; he once again faces A.

◆**18, 19, 20.** B loses no time in gaining the attack initiative. He jumps directly at A and dives down under him in an attempt to pick up A's left leg.

◆**21, 22, 23.** A evades the attack by pulling his left leg free from B's grasp and pivoting around to his left on his right leg; he swings his freed left leg in an arc around to his left, raises his left arm overhead, and prepares to assume *sikap naga.*

21

22

26

27

◆**24, 25.** Before A can assume *sikap naga* B takes decisive action. Upon rising from his crouching posture (◆**23**), he brings his extended left leg under his body, shifts his weight onto that leg and, using it as a platform, delivers the ball of his right foot in a roundhouse kick to A's solar plexus.

Silat Sequence 5

◆**26.** A instantly retaliates and takes decisive action. He turns to his right and steps forward onto his right leg, which he positions in front of the foot of B's platform left leg.

◆**27.** At this instant he delivers the forearm-elbows of both arms in downward chopping fashion against B; his left arm strikes against B's spinal (thoracic) region while his right arm impacts at the base of B's skull. This ends the exercise.

1

2

3

7

8

9

TRAINING EXERCISE 16

Preparation

◆**1.** A (left) steps down from *sikap burung kuntul* onto his right leg and advances on B, who awaits the oncoming attack in *sikap melewis.*

Silat Sequence 1

◆**2, 3.** A leaps forward onto his left leg and delivers a side thrust-kick with the heel of his right foot aimed at the inner area of B's left leg at the knee joint; at the same time he strikes in backhand fashion at B's face using his clenched right fist.

◆**4.** B evades the kick and the blow by stepping backward and to his left with his left leg.

◆**5.** B then shifts his weight onto that leg and, using it as an axle, pivots around to his right; his right leg comes around in an arc behind him.

◆**6.** A assumes *sikap burung kuntul* while B takes *sikap pendeta.*

5

6

11

12

◆7, 8. A attempts decisive action. He turns to his right, stamps his raised right leg to the ground, and, using that leg as a platform, delivers the heel of his left foot in a side thrust-kick aimed at the outer area of B's left leg at the knee joint.

Silat Sequence 2

◆9, 10. Before A can focus the kick B evades it; he turns his body to his left and withdraws his target leg to assume *sikap putri;* A withdraws his kicking left leg and again assumes *sikap burung kuntul.*

◆11. B takes decisive action. He jumps directly at A onto his left leg.

◆12. Using that leg as a platform, B delivers a side thrust-kick under A's raised left leg with the heel of his right foot aimed at the knee joint on the inside of A's platform right leg.

13

14

15

19

20

Silat Sequence 3

◆13, 14. A evades the kick by jumping forward onto his left leg; he then steps forward with his trailing right leg to assume *sikap pendeta;* B retracts his kicking leg and assumes *sikap burung kuntul.*

◆15. Immediately B tries again to take decisive action. He steps forward to the ground on his raised right leg and turns to his right to move against A. Using his right leg as a platform, B delivers a roundhouse kick with the inner anklebone of his left foot aimed at A's groin.

Silat Sequence 4

◆16. A deflects B's kick by using the palms of both hands against the outside of B's kicking leg near the ankle. At the same time, A turns to his left and brings his left leg around in an arc to his left side.

◆17, 18. A then assumes *sikap harimau* while B takes advantage of the force of A's deflection to turn completely around to his right on his platform right leg. As he faces A, B stamps his raised left leg to the ground; he shifts his weight onto that leg and raises his right leg to assume *sikap burung kuntul.*

16

17

18

22

23

◆19. B takes decisive action. He steps forward to the ground with his raised right leg and closes with A; at the same time he delivers a double thrust-punch with both arrowhead fists to the right side of A's head.

Silat Sequence 5

◆20, 21. A suddenly pivots in place, turning to his right and using the palms of both hands to deflect B's punching arms to his right. A assumes *sikap putri* as B takes *sikap pendeta.*

◆22, 23. A takes decisive action. He quickly shifts his weight onto his advanced right leg. Using that leg as a platform, he delivers a crescent kick that impacts the outer anklebone of his left leg against B's solar plexus; at the same time he delivers the fingers of his left hand in whip fashion into B's face to end the exercise.

6 SELF-DEFENSE APPLICATIONS: BELA DIRI

The application of P.D. silat to specific self-defense situations is, in the national Indonesian language, called *bela diri.* Effective technique used at the time of a self-defense emergency derives from the exponent's thorough understanding of and expertise in the fundamentals of P.D. silat. Naturally enough the defender must be completely familiar with the formation of anatomical weapons and the vital target areas for which these weapons are best suited. In addition he must be well grounded in the training exercises presented in chapter 5. The trainee should not attempt the self-defense responses presented below before he has a background in these fundamentals.

The relationship between P.D. training exercises and real combat such as results in the defense of one's life is an obvious one. There is no action or technique in the training exercises that cannot be put to good use in self-defense. But the training exercise is only what its name suggests, a method by which the exponent can train himself to respond correctly to an attack against his person.

We have seen that it is the characteristic of the P.D. training exercise to permit a series of actions and responses to be carried out in a sequence during which each participant has the opportunity to respond in various ways. The length of the multiple-sequence training exercise is intended to develop the exponent's mental alertness and adaptability, his proficiency in making physical responses, and his stamina in protracted action. Self-defense situations, however, are rarely conducive to protracted action. It is usually the nature of the attacker to strike quickly with the intent of rendering his victim helpless. The defender, too, responds with decisive action as quickly as possible, intending that there will be no further aggression on the part of his attacker. The sooner such an effect can be realized the more expert the defender is in self-defense technique.

Yet another difference lies between the training exercises and the self-defense applications. Whereas in the training exercises the role of he who is the attacker and he who is the defender is not clearly defined, since these roles are frequently changed, in self-defense applications there is a very clearly established aggressor.

All self-defense responses demonstrated here are based on the component sequential actions explained in chapter 5. These responses have been specially selected not only because they are representative of the P.D. system, but also because they are simple and direct in nature and are effective against the specific types of attack shown. These responses are quick and efficient methods that anybody can perform after sufficient practice, but they must be used with great discretion as they are capable of causing serious injury or even death to the recipient. It is true that there are other techniques of self-defense that might be used in the emergency situations depicted, but the trainee is advised first to practice what is shown before making any elaborations on his own.

R.M.S. Dirdjoatmodjo, the founder and incumbent spiritualist and master-teacher (pandekar) of the P.D. system, demonstrates and explains all responses in this chapter. When a problem of interpretation occurs the trainee is advised to return to the appropriate earlier chapter in which the fundamentals of the response are described.

DEFENSES MADE BY GOING INSIDE A LUNGE-PUNCH TO THE FACE

The Situation

An assailant approaches as you stand in a natural posture: He obviously intends to do you bodily harm. As he nears you the assailant steps forward onto his right leg and punches at your face with his right fist, as shown in the two figures above.

Response Summary

There are several options open to you if you decide to respond to this kind of attack by going inside the attacker's punching arm, that is, gaining control of that arm by action taken against its inner surfaces as you face the assailant from a position that is directly in front of him.

1

2

3

Response 1

◆1. As the assailant is in the act of punching, shift your weight onto your right leg; raise your left leg, bending it at the knee. At the same time, bring your left arm upward against the inside of his punching arm and use the outer surface of your arm to deflect the assailant's arm outward to your left. Hold your left hand open with the palm upward and the fingers pointing to your left, in the manner of a hook over the assailant's arm. Begin to raise your right arm, bent at the elbow, overhead.

◆2. Deliver a crescent kick and impact the outer edge of your left anklebone against the assailant's ribs on his left side.

◆3. Follow up the kick by delivering a roundhouse loop that cup-impacts your left palm-hand against the assailant's right ear; at the same time form a claw-hand with your right hand and position it at the level of your head on your right side, keeping it ready for instant use if you need it.

1

2

Response 2

This response differs somewhat from that of Response 1 because the assailant is pressing his attack and is much closer to you when he delivers his punch.

◆1. Quickly shift your weight onto your left leg; as you do so, bring your left arm upward along the inside of the attacker's right arm and use the outer surfaces of your arm to deflect the punch outward to your left. Position your left hand, held open with the palm facing upward and the fingers pointing to your left, so that it is hooked over the assailant's arm. Begin to raise your right arm, bent at the elbow, and turn your palm downward.

◆2. Step forward onto your right leg and position your right foot between the assailant's feet; at the same time deliver a right forearm-elbow in driving fashion to strike against the left side of the assailant's face; twist your upper body to the left to reinforce this blow. Keep your left arm and hand in covering position over the assailant's punching right arm.

1

2

3

Response 3

Here the attacker is also crowding you as he punches at your face.

◆**1, 2.** Shift your weight onto your left leg and simultaneously bring your left arm up to the inside of his punching arm in order to use the outer surfaces of your left arm to deflect it outward to your left. Position your left hand, held open with the palm upward and fingers pointing to your left, in hook fashion over the attacker's arm; also raise your right arm, bent at the elbow, overhead. Form a right claw-hand, palm facing the assailant, and bring it to the level of your head on your right side.

◆**3.** Raise your right leg, bend it at the knee, and deliver your knee straight forward and up into your assailant's solar plexus; tear at his face with your right claw-hand.

1

2

3

Response 4
In this case the assailant has punched so quickly at your face that you have no time to maneuver.

◆**1, 2.** Stand firmly in place and quickly bring your left arm upward, inside his punching right arm, in order to deflect it outward to your left with the outer surfaces of your arm; *do not* hook your left hand over the assailant's punching arm. Raise your right hand and form right and left claw-hands, palms facing the assailant.

◆**3.** Keep both feet in place as you tear at his face with either claw-hand, or with both of them in alternating fashion. You may also choose to execute the double eye-gouge.

1 *2*

DEFENSES MADE BY GOING OUTSIDE A LUNGE-PUNCH TO THE FACE

The Situation

An assailant confronts you very quickly from the front and lashes out at your face with a right thrust-punch. You are standing in a natural posture.

Response Summary

If you choose to deal with your assailant by going to the outside of his punching arm, that is, not to stand squarely in front of him, you reduce the chance that he will kick or knee you. There are several good courses of action open to you in making this kind of response.

Response 1

◆1. As your assailant lunges forward onto his right leg to deliver a thrust-punch with his right fist aimed at your face, step a bit to your left side with your left leg and quickly shift your weight onto that leg; at the same time deflect his punching arm to your right by using the palm of your left hand against the outer surface of his punching arm near his elbow. Cover your groin with your right palm.

◆2. Raise your right leg, bend it at the knee, and deliver a snap-kick straight forward to impact the instep of your right foot against your assailant's groin. As you kick bring your left hand into protective position in front of you and continue to cover your groin with your open right hand.

1

2

3

4

2′

3′

Response 2

◆1, 2. In making this defense it is necessary to move in closer to the attacker than you did in the preceding response. Step diagonally forward with your left leg and position your left foot outside and alongside the attacker's advanced right foot. Deflect his punching arm to your right rear corner with your left palm, which makes contact against the outer surfaces of his punching arm near the elbow. Cover your groin with your open right hand.

◆3, 4. After you make this initial evasionary action quickly lower your body by crouching down and, at the same time, deliver a right thrust-punch into the assailant's solar plexus; use your open left hand in a protective role in front of your body at the level of your throat.

Alternate Response 2

◆2′, 3′. This defense is a variation of that shown in Response 2. At the instant that you complete your evasionary move (see ◆2 in Response 2) you may elect to take a different course of action. Instead of crouching down and delivering a right thrust-punch into your attacker's solar plexus you can assume an erect posture and deliver a right arrowhead fist into his throat from underneath his punching right arm.

1

2

3

4

Response 3

This response is difficult to make but it best represents the speed and agility which are characteristic of the trained silat exponent.

◆**1.** As your assailant punches at your face, quickly cross-step your right leg diagonally forward to position your right foot outside and alongside his advanced right foot; at the same time brush his punching arm to your right rear corner by using the palm of your left hand.

◆**2, 3.** Turn to your right and go behind him; step onto your left leg and position your left foot behind his right foot. Quickly shift your weight onto your left leg and raise your right leg, bending it at the knee; at the same time raise both hands, held open, high overhead.

◆**4.** From your position behind the assailant deliver the knife-edge of your right hand to the base of his skull.

1

DEFENSE AGAINST A FRONTAL ARM SEIZURE

The Situation

An assailant has seized your right arm as you stand in a natural posture. He holds it tightly with his right hand gripped atop your wrist; his left hand grips from below your elbow.

Response Summary

Though you might possibly deliver a kick to counter your assailant, the amount of force that he is applying to your captured arm might upset your balance as you kick. Therefore you should choose a different course of action. If he maintains his hold on your arm you may throw him to the ground; if he releases his hold you may strike him.

Response

◆1. Do not resist your assailant as he grips your right arm. Widen your stance a bit, form a fist with your right hand, and keep moderate tension in your captured arm.

2

3

4

5

◆**2, 3.** As he begins to double your arm up and is moving forward along your right side in an attempt to drive your arm up behind your back into a hammer lock, do nothing to resist him. Ready your left fist and position it at your left side near your heart as he comes alongside you.

◆**4.** As your assailant forces your captured arm up behind your back suddenly lower your body and pivot on both feet to turn fully around to your left.

◆**5.** Step forward with your right leg to position your right foot just ahead of your advanced left foot; you now face the same direction as the assailant.

6

7

8

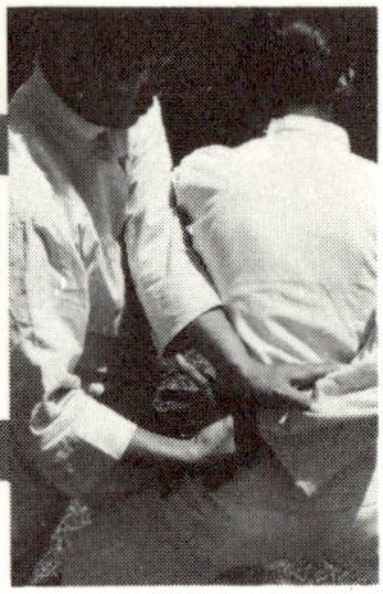

9

10

◆**6, 7.** Quickly shift your weight onto your right leg and step with your left leg to your left side and behind the assailant so that your left foot lies alongside the inside of his outstretched left leg. Crouch down behind him. Your right arm remains doubled up behind your back; keep your left fist at your left side.

◆**8.** Suddenly rise out of your crouch and ram the left side of your body up against the assailant's right side; he continues to hold your right arm with both hands.

◆**9, 10.** Quickly stretch out your left arm across the front of his body at the level of his chest; by swinging your left arm backward against the upper portion of his body you can topple him backward over your extended left leg and hurl him bodily to the ground and onto his head.

5′

6′

7′

8′

9′

10′

Alternate Response

Should your assailant release his two-hand grip on your right arm while you are turning around to your left in preparation for making the throw against him (see ◆**4, 5**), you can deal with him in a different manner.

◆**5′, 6′, 7′.** Just as you complete your turn and are stepping behind the assailant with your left leg in order to close with him and make the throw, you feel him release his double grip on your right arm.

◆**8′, 9′, 10′.** Keep both feet firmly in place, left leg advanced, and immediately deliver your right forearm-elbow in driving fashion against the left side of his face to knock him backward to the ground.

1

2

DEFENSE AGAINST A PUNCHING ATTACK FROM THE REAR

The Situation

An assailant attacks you from a position at your right side and somewhat to the rear. He is delivering a lunge-punch with his right fist aimed at your head just as you catch sight of him.

Response Summary

In making a defense you can either turn outside or inside the attacker's punching arm. Either basic form of response should be suited to the terrain or other factors which will determine your course of action.

Response 1

◆1, 2. As the assailant punches at your head, hold your ground but pivot on both feet and turn to your right. At the same time deflect his punching arm to the right by using your left palm along the outer surfaces of his punching arm near the wrist. Cover your groin with your open right hand. These actions enable you to counter him from a position that is outside his punching right arm.

3

4

5

◆3. Shift your weight forward onto your advanced right leg and quickly raise your left leg, bending it at the knee. At the same time bring your left arm across the front of your body to the left and position your left hand, palm facing the assailant, at the level of your face; bend and raise your right arm upward to the left across the front of your body and hold it at the level of your solar plexus.

◆4. With a sudden movement leap into the air and change leg positions; stand on your left leg as you raise your right leg and bend it at the knee. Raise both hands, palms facing the assailant, high overhead.

◆5. From this position deliver the knife-edge of your right hand in a downward chop to the base of your assailant's skull; keep your right leg ready to deliver a kick should this become necessary.

1

2

3

4

Response 2

◆**1, 2.** In this response you must turn inside the attacker's punching right arm just as he punches at your head from a position behind you. Take a short arc-step backward with your right leg and position your right foot between the feet of the assailant as you turn to the right to face him. Simultaneously, raise both arms in front of your body; use the knife-edge of your left hand against the inner surfaces of his arm near the mid-forearm to misdirect his punch to your left. Raise and bend your right arm to position your open right hand, palm facing downward, at the level of your face.

◆**3, 4.** Cover the punching arm of the assailant with your left hand as you quickly deliver your right forearm-elbow in driving fashion against his throat.

1

2

3

Response 3

◆1. An assailant who is located directly behind you punches at your head just as you catch sight of him. There is no time to maneuver. Quickly shift your weight forward onto your right leg and bend that knee in order to lower your body as you lean well forward, away from the oncoming punch. Keep both hands open and position them in front of you.

◆2, 3. Deliver a reverse sickle-kick that impacts your left heel into your assailant's groin. Then immediately swing your left forearm-elbow to the rear in backhand fashion so that your arm passes beneath his outstretched punching arm; strike against his right pectoral muscle.

1

2

3

4

Response 4

◆**1.** An assailant comes up behind you. You catch sight of him at the instant he delivers a lunge-punch with his right fist against your head.

◆**2, 3.** Turn to your left, inside his punching arm, and face him; at the same time deflect his punching arm by bringing the outer surfaces of your left arm against his inner right arm. Quickly shift your weight onto your left leg, raising your right leg and bending it at the knee; simultaneously ready your right arrowhead fist and position it at the level of your chest.

◆**4.** Deliver your right arrowhead fist into the assailant's throat. If you are close enough to your assailant or if you can pull him forward by the action of your left hand against his punching arm, also deliver your right knee straight up into his solar plexus.

1

2

3

DEFENSE AGAINST A BUTTING ATTACK MADE FROM THE REAR

The Situation

An assailant has come up unnoticed behind you as you stand in a natural posture. He steps between your legs from the rear with his left leg and positions his left foot between your feet. He butts the left side of his body up against your right rear side in an attempt to spill you forward to the ground; he is applying pressure against your right thigh with both hands to forestall any kicking action that you might try to make against him.

Response Summary

Because this attack comes without warning and the force being applied is sending you forward and off-balance, your best choice is to blend with the attack and execute a countertechnique from a position on the ground.

Response

◆**1, 2, 3.** As the attacker drives his body against yours, evade the main force of his drive by turning quickly to your left.

4

5

6

7

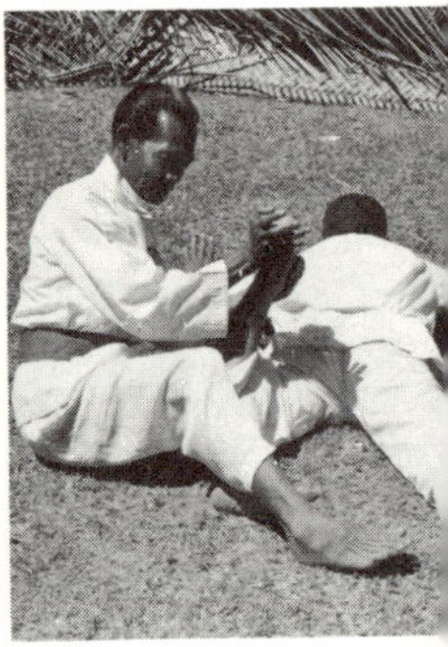

8

◆4, 5. Dive for the ground and support yourself on both hands; keep your left knee bent and raised and kneel down on your right knee. As you stabilize your position on the ground turn your head to the left in order to catch sight of the assailant.

◆6. Sit down on your right buttock, turn to your left and, at the same time, bring your right thigh close up against the front inner surface of your attacker's left ankle. Hook your left leg over his outstretched left leg just in back of his left knee joint.

◆7. By turning to your left you can exert a shearing force against your assailant's trapped left leg. Turn with enough force so that your action combined with the attacker's forward motion in his attempt to flee sends him sprawling face down to the ground. Assume a sitting posture.

◆8. Before your assailant can recover make him submit by raising and bending his left leg as you apply leverage against his ankle and toes with your two hands.

1

2

DEFENSE AGAINST A LEG SEIZURE FROM THE SIDE

The Situation

You are standing in a natural posture when an assailant suddenly jumps at you from your right side. He steps with his left leg across the front of your right leg and dives down to seize the ankle of your right leg with his right hand extended between his legs. Hé attempts to pick up your right leg and hurl you backward to the ground.

Response Summary

You catch sight of your attacker just as he dives for your legs. He is pulling your right leg with his right hand and is, at the same time, pushing you backward with his left forearm. He is also in position to use his legs in crab-scissors fashion against your body should you resist him. You therefore choose to blend with his attack and counter him from a standing position.

Response

◆1, 2. As the assailant begins to pull and lift your right leg stand firm by shifting your weight over that leg. Permit him to move that leg a bit forward.

3

4

5

◆**3, 4, 5.** Suddenly shift the position of your trapped right leg. Do this by turning your body a bit to your left and slipping your right knee in that direction.

◆**6, 7.** As your knee slips free from contact with the back of his left leg, twist back to your right and drive your weight forward by lunging over your right leg. Exert pressure with your right knee and shin against the calf of the attacker's left leg. This action traps his leg; apply sufficient pressure and send him sprawling face down to the ground. At the same time deliver both arrowhead fists in thrust-punches into his left kidney region. Cause the assailant to submit in a prone position by pressing your right knee and shin down along the back surface of his left knee joint (kneel down hard). Keep your balance and remain ready for instant action should he attempt to continue his aggression.

7

GLOSSARY-INDEX